Reboot
Your
Business

STEPHEN SACKS

Reboot Your Business

Copyright Stephen Sacks © 2018

ISBN 978-1-912009-2-13
First Published by Compass-Publishing 2018
www.compass-publishing.com

Printed in the United Kingdom

A catalogue version of the book can be found at the British Library

Designed and edited by The Book Refinery Ltd
www.thebookrefinery.com

This publication is designed to provide accurate and authoritative information for business owners. It is sold under the express understanding that any decisions or actions you take as a result of reading this book must be based on your commercial judgement and will be at your sole risk. The author will not be held responsible for the consequences of any actions and/or decisions taken as a result of any information given or recommendations made.

What Clients Say About Working With Stephen

"Stephen is one of those rare people that can inspire and help get the best out of you.

I have found him to be an honest and trustworthy individual who I can rely upon at all times.

I like bouncing ideas off him as he is a highly professional and open-minded person with an exceptional depth of knowledge in business solutions.

I have the pleasure of working with Stephen on a joint venture project and I am looking forward to our ongoing business adventures."

Michele Yianni - Director - Kyle Macy Property Solutions Limited

"Stephen provides inspiration to many businesses. He is insightful and energetic. He questions deeply, identifies issues and then insists on massive action in order to move his clients on. I know that there are a number of businesses that would have folded without his lead that not only turned the corner but in fact went on to much success. If Reboot Your Business creates only 1% of the value that Stephen does with his clients one-to-one that will offer readers a multi-fold return on their investment in purchasing it."

Rupert Honywood - MD - Integrated Marketing Bureau

"I have known Stephen for many years and am always amazed by his business acumen and ability to reinvent himself in business. Someone I truly look up to and follow as best as I can!"

Jason Conway - MD - Ameris Ltd

"As founder of The Supper Club I have had, over its 15-year history, the good fortune to meet and learn from some of Britain's greatest entrepreneurial talent: Stephen is one of those amazing businessmen. Home to nearly 500 of Britain's most successful 'scale-up' founders and CEOs, the Club's members are committed to helping each other grow personally as well as commercially. As a long standing member, over ten years, Stephen absolutely personifies the Club's values and its key principal of 'Give and Get'. His wealth of experience as leader of a number of successful businesses means he's been able to help dozens of others with timely advice and inspiration over the years. I am absolutely delighted that Stephen is now able to share this wealth of experience with a far wider audience and that I have a chance to thank him more publicly."

Duncan Cheatle - Founder & Chairman - The Supper Club

"Only entrepreneurs truly understand entrepreneurs. That's why, as an entrepreneur, I appreciate having Stephen as an advisor. He is smart and savvy. He is a problem identifier and solver. He is relentless in pursuing the goals he agrees he will deliver with his clients. He remains loyal to the vision and the belief. He challenges and probes – but always with a win outcome. It's tough and lonely being an entrepreneur and it's important to surround yourself with the right people. Stephen is someone I am proud to have in my squad."

David CM Carter - Founder & Chairman - QDOOZ

"Stephen, or 'Poker Face' as I affectionately refer to him, is not a man to pull any punches and he doesn't have a calling in international diplomacy, but he most certainly is someone you want on your team. Clear-thinking, straight-talking and fairly funny to boot, Stephen identifies areas where a slightly different approach may unlock cash in your business, improve your profitability and put you on a completely fresh trajectory. It is, quite simply, the difference between working *on* your business instead of working *in* your business."

Oliver Codrington - Clinic Director - London Wellness Centre Limited

"The thing about Stephen is his immediate intuition of the right thing to do, the best way to do it and his no-nonsense approach to helping you get it done. Well worth the time of day!"

William Gets - MD - Brainstorm Marketing

Dedication

For my girls, Georgia, Juliette, Amelia and Josie and my beautiful wife, Harriet who inspire me every day.

And my parents, Wally and Gwenda - it's just a shame my dad is no longer around to read it!

Foreword

by Julian Birkinshaw, Professor and Deputy Dean, London Business School

I've been working with, advising and researching small businesses for 25 years, and over this time I've figured out some important rules of thumb about what makes them tick – why some thrive while others stumble and fall.

It goes without saying that you need a high-energy entrepreneur to get a small business started. Tenacity and optimism are hugely important character traits, and being able to convey an exciting vision to others, so that they want to get involved, is also pretty central. It's often said that entrepreneurship is the pursuit of opportunity beyond the resources you control – so knowing how to tap into those resources you need is a big piece of the puzzle.

Do you need to have a unique value proposition? Or to develop a piece of intellectual property that you alone have access to? These are great to have, but not essential. There are plenty of successful start-up companies that aren't completely unique in how they are positioned or in what they sell. Such companies just find themselves a niche and work hard to keep others at bay.

And what about being single-minded in pursuit of a specific goal? We applaud James Dyson for his dogged determination in developing a bagless vacuum cleaner after 5,000 failed prototypes. But it turns out that being able to refocus and pivot, as we say these days, is just as important as sticking to an original vision. Most successful entrepreneurs shifted direction many times in their early years, especially those who were trying to create a growth business rather than occupy a small niche. From Richard Branson to Elon Musk to Mark Zuckerberg: all of them had their share of failures and false starts.

These observations provide a framing for *Reboot Your Business* in a couple of ways: first, Stephen Sacks is your quintessential entrepreneur.

He has built and run more businesses than I can count. He's had his share of setbacks. He's shown huge resilience and tenacity. He knows more about the ups and downs of the small businessperson than anyone else I know. His insights and words of wisdom are well worth listening to.

Second, if you want to grow and to push your business in a new direction, you need some fresh thinking. That's what this book provides: not just great examples of businesses Stephen has founded or worked with; and not just his reflections on the difficult challenges you face in developing your business further; but really practical advice as well, about sources of funding, tax credit schemes, agencies that can help you, and so on.

No business book will ever give you *the* answer to where your next growth opportunity will come from. By definition, that's your problem to solve and it's unique to the market you're working in and your personal circumstances. Instead, this book gives you lots of answers – insights that will spark new opportunities, lessons from experience, and frameworks that will help you organise your thoughts. The rest is up to you.

A Note From The Author

This book is written in three sections. The first challenges the SME business owner to consider their venture through the changes that are impacting us all as progress gets faster and mediocrity gets left behind. The second is about how to raise cash. The final section is a week-by-week programme aimed at making incremental improvements. This book also includes online tools.

Contents

Part 3 - How to Play - 173

Introduction

Dear SME owner,

Congratulations – you've already achieved more than most people ever do in their lives! Most people can only dream about the opportunity of running their own business but you are actually doing it.

Ideas are two-a-penny quite frankly, but that's where most concepts stay – as ideas. Very few see the light of day as businesses and most of those are stillborn on the kitchen table. If I had a pound for every person who tells me about what they want to start, could have started, did start but failed at, then I wouldn't be spending my time writing books on business and consulting with businesses. I'd be too busy spending all those pounds.

However, your achievement, impressive though it is, is statistically (and rather depressingly) probably fleeting at best. The fact is that the average business has less life in it than the average dog. Sadly, 80% of businesses fail within five years and of the 20% still standing, 80% of those statistically will fail in a further five years. As the more numerate amongst you will already have worked out, 20% of 20% is just 4% – yes, a measly 4% survive ten years. That's 96% failure. I mean, come on, these are precious entities that have tied up people's lives, cash and dreams for years and they are just dropping like flies. It seems crazy, doesn't it?

Why does it happen?

And how can you prevent it happening to your business?

These are the two questions that this book sets out to answer, and if you can't answer these two questions as a business owner, then you may be steering your own ship at the moment, but ultimately you will be steering it as effectively as Captain Edward John Smith steered his. And he managed to drive the Titanic into an iceberg. Interestingly, the activity of organising the deck chairs on the Titanic as a strategy to try to calm passengers and remove their focus from the lack of lifeboats, has become a famous metaphor for all activities with no real benefits. This is, however, the description that best sums up the groundhog-day way in which most leaders that I see are operating their ventures.

Generally, that's why I get called in, because of the realisation that they are still running round the same hamster wheel. But guess what? Little Johnny has a new pet now and he doesn't really care about his hamster anymore. The chances are, of course, that little Johnny has actually discovered tech or social media and that explains the recent lack of activity in your hamster cage. Basically, the world has moved on and whatever strategies were working before just aren't working so well now.

In years gone by, of course, it was often enough that your great-great-great-grandfather had started a butcher's shop or suchlike in your local village back in the day, and that was handed down through the generations until it reached you. However, with the virtual exception of the Windsors, family business continuity doesn't really work so well these days. Actually, scratch that. Even the Windsors had to rebrand in 1917 from the Saxe-Coburgs, as German brands just weren't so popular in the UK at that time for some reason!

Generally in life, if you start out at something – like a sport, for example – you practise a lot, improve and get more competitive; you then start winning medals and ultimately have the opportunity to retire a champion. And that's how it used to be in business. But no more, alas.

Today, getting to the top of your game isn't very helpful since the 'game' and its rules are likely to change between the time you start and before you get to the top. In fact, getting to the top of your game can even be a decided disadvantage. It can blindside you to the external changes that are occurring that may make your whole business model redundant before you even get close to really monetising it.

I mean, who would want to be the leader today in camera film like Kodak, the leader in cathode ray TVs like Sony, the leader in mobile telephony like Nokia or the leader in mobile email like Blackberry? No one, of course, because virtually all these industries have been destroyed by one new industry – that of the smart phone!

The first Apple iPhone was released, amazingly enough, as recently as mid-2007, and that changed everything. Nowadays the ubiquitous ownership and total domination of people's time and lives by the smart phone has changed the way we all need to do business, and so have all the other industries that it has spawned: apps, streaming, e-commerce etc etc. All businesses need to uprate their business model to succeed in the age of the smart phone and in the age of faster and faster changing markets and demands.

This book is designed to be both thought-provoking and practical. It's thought-provoking in the way that I have set out each chapter, asking interesting and probing questions – perhaps questions that you haven't asked yourself before (or have been afraid to ask). It's important that you answer these because, if you don't, then you'll be like all the other small business owners out there who don't get it and wonder why their business disappoints.

There are three sections. The first is a broad look at the opportunities and challenges of running a business in the twenty-first century. The second part is a guide to where the modern entrepreneur can find more capital that will both cushion the business from shocks as well as provide the money to launch new and hopefully relevant ideas onto the market; ideas that will keep the business prospering through ongoing trial and error. The third is a provoking, week-by-week plan that, if followed, will guide a business to make ongoing changes to the enterprise designed to progressively squeeze increasing efficiency that will, over time, revolutionise the results that the business produces. There is also space in this section for you to add your own notes as you consider how to implement the actions.

The book is practical because, not only have I included case studies that look at the various issues set out in each chapter, but there are also week-by-week action points for you to engage with, which hopefully ask and encourage you to answer some deep and probing questions, just as a mentor or a coach would. Some easy-to-complete worksheets are available online too, so filling these in will be simple and quick. Don't forget that it's only ACTION that gets results; if you decide not to engage with the action points, then don't expect anything different to happen.

Once you've thought about, planned and strategised a new type of business based on what you have today, I direct you to places where you can raise the capital you need from free sources. This is the primary difference between this book and almost every other business book you could choose. Not only do I help you to focus your internal resources on the areas that will profit you the most, I also advise you on how and where to raise the funds necessary to fulfil your plans, often without incurring either debt or additional shareholders.

In addition, as with the worksheets already mentioned, there are web-based tools readers can access that have been designed to complement the written material.

The intellectual property that differentiates Funding Nav from all other business consultancy concepts is the notion of 'free cash'. I try to be as helpful as possible here in assisting you to negotiate the free cash options available to you, but I also welcome email enquiries from readers direct at stephen.sacks@fundingnav.com. I can then consider your own business's position and advise you on an appropriate course of action. Normally I charge an absolute minimum of £2k per day for consulting or advising but, because you bought this book, there is absolutely no charge to you for contacting me with any questions that reading it raises. My goal is to help as many readers as possible achieve a high level of personal satisfaction and financial freedom from actioning the ideas featured. I would like in some small way to be a catalyst to your success!

The book is designed to be read from cover to cover, and then kept on your desk as a reference point for you to dip in and out of in the future. You'll also be able to revisit the resources available at www.fundingnav. com.

So, since you have invested some money and you are about to invest some of your time in reading this book, I would implore you to:

1. Really think about some of the points that are made here.

2. Allow your ideas to develop.

3. Not be afraid of confronting the elephant in the room regardless of how painful that might seem at the outset.

4. Take soundings from people you trust who will be honest with you.

5. Take action.

If you don't agree with some of what I have to say, that's fair enough and please feel free to send me feedback. But, honestly, this book cost literally millions of pounds in real-time research, through errors I've made or that others made before hitting on the right path – so excuse me if I take your feedback with a pinch of salt. What I'm actually much more interested in than your unsolicited point of view is your real-life experience in trying out some of the ideas and concepts set out here, and the improvement you were hopefully able to make as a result of reading and acting on what you read. I'm especially interested in examples where you can monetise the result as that's what I'm really trying to achieve here:

Measurable, positive impact on my readers' business outcomes and resultant improvement in their lives.

PART 1

The State of Play

1

Rules of the Game

Moore's Law has changed everything!

In 1965, which is coincidentally the same year that I was born, Gordon Moore, the co-founder of Intel, noticed that the number of transistors per square inch on integrated circuit boards was doubling every year since their invention, and consequently doubling computer power and halving the cost. He predicted that this trend would continue indefinitely. Whilst he wasn't quite right as the time taken to double expanded from 12 to 18 months, he was nonetheless almost right and has been continually proved right over the last half century.

The promise that software is eating the world is actually now a well-founded reality, and so every organisation is becoming a digital organisation. Technology is the primary line item on every business initiative's critical path. That means the enterprise is only as effective as its IT organisation. But there's a problem: these companies know that often traditional IT operating models aren't able to meet the demands of this changing clock speed.

What's behind this?

1. There is competitive pressure. Competition is coming from everywhere – not only from traditional competitors but from new entrants seemingly appearing out of nowhere. Who knew, ten years ago, that Amazon, an online book-seller, would one day become the industry heavyweight in cloud infrastructure?

2. There are more tools than ever that organisations can leverage
    to transform their businesses. With IoT, SaaS, big data, social,
    mobile, cloud and APIs ('big 7 technology drivers'), they have
    more innovation opportunities, more new product ideas, and
    more new channels they can take advantage of.

These technology drivers are forcing a dramatic acceleration in what
businesses can and should do to remain competitive and relevant. How
nimble and responsive should you be?

In August 2016, I took my family on a road trip from Houston, Texas
across the USA. The first place we visited on the tour was the *NASA
Christopher C. Kraft Jr. Mission Control Centre* in Houston. Building
Number 30 contains the iconic control centre itself that was operational
from 1965 until 1992. This room represented the peak of technical
achievement when it was built and, whilst it obviously developed over
the period of time that it was operational, it has now been restored to
its original state. It looked a bit like an expanded flight deck from the
USS Enterprise as seen in the original *Star Trek* series featuring William
Shatner. This isn't really surprising as the series was shot at the same time
in the late 1960s, and this thinking represented the absolute pinnacle of
current technology.

Houston Mission Control is dominated by banks and banks of small
cathode ray screens set into desks without keyboards or mice, but with a
profusion of knobs and buttons. It looks so quaint today, and it is amazing
that only 50 years ago the peak of man's space exploration achievements,
including Apollo, Gemini and Sky Lab, was being run from a facility like
this. The most amazing thing, which is a real example of the impact of
Moore's Law, is that the overall size of the facility is vast, the majority
of the space being taken up with three cavernous halls containing vast
– and I really mean gargantuan – mainframe computers that supported
this infrastructure. Today, a modern BMW that costs a few tens of
thousands has more computing power under its bonnet as standard than
this enormous organisation had at its disposal 50 years ago at a cost of
billions.

Computing power that is doubling every 18 months to two years, whilst human intelligence remains static at best, means that whole industries will be born and will die in our lifetimes. When I was born in the 1960s, not only were the world's biggest businesses, Apple, Microsoft, Facebook and Google, not yet born, but even their very concepts and industries would have been unfathomable to most people who weren't avid readers of science fiction at that time. So much of what was literally science fiction when I was a kid is now fairly humdrum and affordable kit that has become pretty ubiquitous today.

Computing power may now (only) be doubling every 18 months, but the impact on other areas of society is similarly speeding up. We are now in the sharing economy, largely facilitated by technology but necessitated by a backward step in wealth: millennials become the first generation to be less wealthy than their parents, as society pays the price for the unaffordable pensions and healthcare promised to all after the Second World War.

Not since Adam and Eve had Cain and Abel has the sheer volume of humanity doubled in a lifetime, and we march on towards eight billion up from just four billion in 1970. Populations in the mature economies of the west stagnate whereas those in growth economies such as India explode. These countries have a burgeoning middle class, stretching resources like power generation, food production and infrastructure beyond what seemed possible only recently. Our ingeniousness in pushing the envelope is moving ahead of our growing needs all the time.

In the west, we have been exporting low-value manufacturing jobs to cheaper and cheaper labour cost countries in a worldwide movement that has been largely positive for the distribution of wealth and the general level of peace and harmony. However, it's not been so good for the environment as we have invented a throwaway economy that has spread from Styrofoam coffee cups to discount clothing so cheap that it can literally be worn once before being discarded.

Now we are starting to export white-collar jobs overseas too, with accountants and lawyers following call centre operators into Bangalore and Manila.

Next will be the march of the robots and Artificial Intelligence. Call centre operators, taxi and truck drivers, doctors and accountants are all professions that will become increasingly redundant over the next few years as smart technology learns these largely mechanical tasks, and whole industry employment areas literally collapse. It's rather like what happened in the agricultural and industrial revolutions in farming, and then in cottage industries as factories and mechanisation took over. It will be fascinating to see what new industries and professions rise up to replace the ones that will inevitably die.

Artificial Intelligence is rapidly developing and is already starting to change the world at a pace that is worrying to some experts. Huge personalities in the tech industry often lament the dangers of unfettered development of AI systems: people like Elon Musk and the late Stephen Hawking, who have warned of a future where AI reigns supreme. Whether or not their concerns are unfounded, there certainly is massive value in keeping a close eye on the progress of AI innovation for the entrepreneur.

AI is getting really good and, in a lot of cases, way better than experts imagined. *AlphaGo*, Google's game playing AI, has been beating the world's best players for a while now, something that wasn't thought to be possible for at least a decade. Elon Musk's *OpenAI* is doing even better than that by beating the world's greatest eSports players at *DOTA 2*, a game that is much more complex than chess and involves tricking opponents. It's easy to see how an argument can be made that we need to more closely and accurately map the development of AI systems.

There is an abundance of almost everything in the market today! Thanks to the likes of Amazon, we can now have what we want, how we want it, when we want it and at the price we want to pay for it. As consumers, we can make our preferences and experiences clear to companies through social media. Each of us is able to broadcast widely, building a level playing field between businesses and consumers.

There is, however, a growing divergence of earnings between the least well paid and the best paid, as few now control the work of many and are able instead to leverage through technology. Bill Gates has suggested that robots should be taxed at the same rate as the human labour they displace in order to deal with the looming issues of under employment and longer lifespans. It's not easy to see how that might work without severely disincentivising human progress, but almost certainly governments will need to adjust to the new realities in the same way as individuals will.

One of the best-known commentators on inequality is Professor Joe Stiglitz from *Columbia Business School*. He told **BBC News** that the problem of increasing inequality was not just to do with lack of training and education.

"What we've seen, particularly in the last 15 years, is that even those who are college graduates have seen their incomes stagnate. The real problem is the rules of the game are stacked for the monopolists, the CEOs [chief executives] of corporations.

"CEOs today get pay that's roughly 300 times that of ordinary workers – it used to be 20 or 30 times. No increase in productivity justifies this change in relative compensation."

Behind the OECD (*Organisation for Economic Co-operation and Development*) averages, there is a considerable range in the degrees of inequality in each country.

One of the report's authors, Mark Pearson from the OECD, told **BBC News**: *"It's not just income that we're seeing being very concentrated – you look at wealth and you find that the bottom 40% of the population in rich countries have only 3% of household wealth whereas the top 10% have over half of household wealth.*

"So that combination of both wealth and income being very concentrated, it means there is no equality of opportunity in many societies and that undermines our growth."

Companies and brands are diverging too between the luxury branded market and the mass-market commoditisation. The mid-market is increasingly a more difficult area to occupy. Ultimately, consumers are polarised between brand and price and, unlike before, corporations cannot easily pigeon hole their consumers into neat socio-economic groups. Nowadays, it is quite likely that a student will afford the most expensive new smart phone whereas a very wealthy person might give up car ownership altogether, especially if they live in an urban centre. Politics are changing too and the old left/right schism is increasingly redundant as the electorate finds itself split more on a geographic and age basis.

Multi-national businesses have for some years enjoyed an almost unfair advantage as they are able to leverage their size and buying power, which includes the country they ultimately deign to pay tax in. Brands like Starbucks, Zara, McDonalds and Amazon crush their competitors across all markets with very little variation to their central proposition.

The gig economy is calling an end to industrialisation as knowledge workers increasingly gravitate out from organised workplaces into shared offices and the free Wi-Fi at Starbucks. They're moving away from unionised collectivisation towards self-reliance and back to the cottage-industry economy of pre-industrialisation, but this time armed with laptops rather than cotton-spinning machines. This movement again is ultimately eroding living standards for most millennials, as they lose the security, sick pay and pension rights that their baby boomer parents enjoyed.

Interestingly though, in the same way that the agricultural and industrial revolutions increased the living standards of mankind as a whole, whilst at the cost of reducing the living standards of most individuals, the tech revolution may well be reversing that by re-empowering the individual at the expense of the corporation.

No doubt, then, that today we are living through exceptional times as consumers, as workers and as citizens. However, for small business owners, the opportunities and threats that now exist to their enterprises are equally without precedent and increasing in scale over time, with change only likely to accelerate things. This means that these three uncomfortable truths that have always been present are now critical if the enterprise is to survive and prosper.

The Three Uncomfortable Truths

1. The only entitlement is opportunity

The world doesn't owe you or your business a living. The opportunity is out there, as it is for us all, but it is your job as a leader to both recognise and then to take that opportunity. Businesses that rely on strapline claims of longevity or succession will flounder, as these claims are increasingly irrelevant to modern consumers. Leaders need to regularly overhaul their central proposition to ensure that it remains both relevant and sticky to their current and potential customers. Businesses should be constantly trialling and testing tweaks to their offer, rolling them out where they prove to be popular and quickly canning them when they are not, to keep things fresh and relevant. They should remove assumption from their planning as much as possible, as ultimately customers vote with their wallets with little concern for what the business thinks.

2. Your business must have at least one unique reason to exist

At one time, for example, being the only speciality store in a town was enough to ensure success, but of course now you will be competing with the out-of-town-category killer and numerous internet retailers, all of whom are capable of offering longer opening hours and cheaper prices than the local store. Good service is a pre-requisite so that won't work as a USP either. The only area that the small business can rely on in the face of competition today is in building a brand based on exceptional service and specialisation. Essentially, SME businesses need to focus on the needs of the core customer and others like them and wrap that in an unbeatable and personalised approach. An example of this would be a restaurant where the client has his own table, wine and food preferences acknowledged and remembered, and receives communications from the restaurant on significant dates (such as birthdays and anniversaries), with relevant deals so that it's actually difficult to even consider going anywhere else, regardless of their pricing and selection.

3. Cash is king

Leaders of businesses that are run with insufficient working capital because they failed to raise an adequate level at the outset, they are overtrading or they are losing money, are prone to making poor long-term decisions as their decision-making process is driven by short-term opportunism and fear. Surviving day-to-day is debilitating and defocusing, and normally disastrous if not dealt with as a priority.

So, there you have it. Change your thinking to reflect the demands of the future rather than the tribulations of the past. It's really important to understand that thinking you have an entitlement to business (when really you DON'T) is a sure-fire way to lose everything. Don't forget that people need to know why they should do business with YOU (and not just visit the next search entry on Google), and you need to have the cash to be there for them.

Key Points

- » No place for arrogance or a false sense of entitlement.
- » Retain a childish fascination in everything tech because it will have an impact on your business whatever industry you're in.
- » Keep trialling and reinventing.
- » Create a USP, retain it and develop it.
- » Don't run out of cash.

2

It's All About You

Most businesses are set up as small enterprises by technicians or enthusiasts, and most businesses then stay that way as an effective vehicle for self-employment.

In the UK, which is probably pretty typical, 99.9% of all businesses (5.4m) are SMEs, and 76% of all businesses employ a maximum of one person and never grow beyond that.

Within five years, 80% of businesses fail, according to Forbes, and 96% fail within ten years.

Obviously some churn is positive for the economy and the natural order of things, but surely something is wrong when 96% of enterprises have shorter lives than the average dog?

So the question is, *why do businesses fail?* And the short answer is that businesses mostly fail because of the **behaviour of the leader** – which is exactly the same reason why businesses ultimately succeed, because success is basically behavioural, not attitudinal or metaphysical.

Behaviours Most Likely to Help the Leader Succeed

1. Hunger

No question. How badly do you want it? Third generation family businesses normally flounder because the first generation came from nothing and created a platform, and the second generation spent their childhood witnessing their parents struggle. The third generation, on the other hand, were born into plenty, are therefore less motivated than their parents and grandparents, and as a result normally wind up closing the doors on the family enterprise.

2. Energy

Make no mistake, the journey to success is *not* for the faint-hearted. Successful entrepreneurs often have very little work/life balance. Even the term *'work/life balance'* is meaningless to them because it suggests that, like most job slaves, you need to trade hours of your life that you love for hours of work that you hate in order to make an income that helps you enjoy your non-work life. However, successful behaviour is viewed by outsiders as being a workaholic: someone who is so in love with what they do that they are addicted to it, they love it and it energises them. Not working is actually dull by comparison; social situations and holidays can be boring and unwelcome interludes to the crusade of their life, which is their business. This may lead to relationship issues but these are often viewed as a price worth paying.

3. Autonomy

Good leaders take on board views but ultimately *make up their own minds*; they are unaffected by unsolicited criticism and treat naysayers with disdain. Strong leaders attract criticism like water attracts ducks but, like ducks in water, it doesn't even come close to ruffling their feathers. They remain strong and are quite prepared to subject themselves to uncomfortable situations that would phase most people in order to achieve their goals. George Bernard Shaw famously said, *"The reasonable man adapts himself to the world; the unreasonable one persists in trying to adapt the world to himself. Therefore, all progress depends on the unreasonable man."*

4. Responsibility

Successful leaders take *responsibility* for their and the team's errors and make sure that they are a learning experience. They make whatever changes are necessary and go again. They are also prepared to share responsibility for success in order to motivate their team.

5. Resilience

The ability to *keep coming back* from failure to ultimately succeed, however many times and however long it takes. Walt Disney, Henry Ford, Conrad Hilton, JC Penney, Sam Walton and HJ Heinz are just a few of the mega successful businessmen who experienced bankruptcy on their way to success. Not to mention Donald Trump, of course, who only escaped personal bankruptcy through his use of corporate insolvency processes. In Silicon Valley today, part of the investment criteria of many funders means that those that have not yet experienced a disaster find it more difficult to attract investment. Funders want to see that the custodian of their investment doesn't experience a first failure on their watch, and has the personality traits to come back from setbacks. Regrettably, we are not so forward thinking in the UK, which is probably why the nine most valuable businesses in the world are American and the tenth is Chinese.

6. Rebelliousness

Successful businesses *take on the establishment and disrupt it to their advantage.* Their leaders are prepared to tackle and challenge authority and the status quo. The skills necessary to succeed in corporate life, which are about recognising and working the hierarchy, are the total antithesis of the skills required to grow an enterprise. These latter skills are about recognising the hierarchy, ambushing it and ultimately destroying it – or perhaps not even recognising it in the first place. Entrepreneurs are prepared to take on the establishment in creative ways.

When Kenneth Cole was starting out in the shoe business, he wanted to show his wares at NY Fashion Week but couldn't afford a catwalk show as the rent and other costs were very high. He did, however, have a large trailer and chose to do a static show in the trailer rather than in a building, thus saving costs. He decided that the best location to site the trailer for the week was on Fifth Avenue (where else?), but the parking regulations are obviously highly restrictive for cars on that street, never mind large trailers.

Cole contacted the City Hall to ask for permission and was rejected out of hand. He persisted and this time asked a different question: *"If anyone would, then who would be allowed to park a trailer on Fifth Avenue for the week, and in what circumstance?"* The answer was that the sole exception to the rule was for the purposes of film production. Cole called back a few minutes later from the *Kenneth Cole Film Production Company*, which he had just incorporated, and got a permit to park his trailer for the week as if to shoot the documentary, *'The Making of a Shoe Company'*.

On the opening day of Fashion Week, Cole had fake camera operators and technicians milling around with no film in their cameras, and the general hubbub attracted a huge swathe of buyers onto the 'set' to look at the collection and place orders. The rest, of course, is history, and the brand has gone from success to success.

Don't prostitute yourself! You have the almost unique opportunity of guiding your own life and making your own choices, free from the influence of overburdening authority that most workers are faced with. So don't throw it all away in an effort to fulfill someone else's dream or destiny. Remember to make your own bed the way you like it – after all, you're the one who's going to lie in it. If you love your work then you'll never work a day in your life. If you don't, however, then you will ultimately fail because success relies in a large part on your ongoing fascination and love for your enterprise, and your willingness to subject yourself to total immersion: nurturing it and thinking about it in a positive way all the time in your subconscious; even when asleep.

In one of the best-thought-out studies on what makes successful businesses *Good To Great*, Jim Collins says that, *"good is the enemy of great"*. What he means is that, if things are OK then, as humans, we tend to leave them be. The problem is that 'OK' is a relative concept and, rather like the frog that doesn't notice when it is slowly being boiled alive, we tend not to consider changing until things get really bad, by which time often it's too late.

Just as a marriage can go stale over time, your relationship with your business can similarly stagnate. The difference between your dissatisfied spouse and your unloved business, however, is that your spouse is likely to give you honest feedback and file for divorce, whereas your business will absorb all sorts of abuse and a lack of love for a time because it can't speak to you.

However, the entity that is your business cannot exist in a vacuum for long, and the contrast between the performance of an unloved business and its more spirited competitors will soon become apparent in lower profits, and then in no profits or even losses. This will, of course, only serve to reinforce and exacerbate the emotional disconnect that led to the issue in the first instance. Whilst, in the speeded-up world in which we live today, all of this will start slowly, after reaching a tipping point, it will begin to work against you in quick time.

So I cannot stress enough that, nowadays, *good isn't just the enemy of great – it just isn't good enough!* Only **great** businesses, the ones with an engaged and motivated leader, can survive in today's market.

The key success factor, even more than innate talent, must be love for what you do, because that is what will ultimately motivate you to direct all your discretionary effort in the general direction of your venture.

Your leadership style might be unusual or even variable, but all that matters really is that you are engaged and authentic, and ultimately that you get results.

A leader's singular job at the end of the day is to get results. But even with all the leadership training programmes and 'expert' advice available, effective leadership still eludes many people and organisations. One reason for this, says Daniel Goleman of *The Harvard Business Review*, is that such experts offer advice based on inference, experience and instinct, not on quantitative data. Now, drawing on research of more than 3,000 executives, Goleman explores which precise leadership behaviours yield positive results. He outlines six distinct leadership styles, each one springing from different components of emotional intelligence. Each style has a specific effect on the working atmosphere of a company, division or team, and, in turn, on its financial performance. The styles, by name and brief description alone, will resonate with anyone who leads, is led, or, as is the case with most of us, does both. Coercive leaders demand immediate compliance. Authoritative leaders mobilise people toward a vision. Affiliative leaders create emotional bonds and harmony. Democratic leaders build consensus through participation. Pacesetting leaders expect excellence and self-direction. And coaching leaders develop people for the future.

The research indicates that leaders who get the best results don't rely on just one leadership style; they use most of the styles in any given week. Goleman details the types of business situations each style is best suited for, and he explains how leaders who lack one or more styles can expand their repertories. He maintains that practice leaders can switch leadership styles to produce powerful results, thus turning the art of leadership into a science.

Key Points

» Falling out of love with your business is the beginning of the end: if you don't love your business then you won't give it all that it takes. In which case change it or change you.

» Use your business as a vehicle to take you on a voyage of change and discovery.

» If you have a setback, get over it! Learn, reset and move on.

» 80/20: there is only one of you, so make sure that you spend most of your time working on the aspects of the business that have 80% of the impact, rather than being a busy fool by sweating the small stuff.

» Talking of 80/20, try to direct 80% of your effort towards the parts of the business that are responsible for 80% of the results, so that it has the biggest impact.

» Vary your style and approach.

3

Get on the Bus

The best leaders are effective *delegators*. They recognise that they have to surround themselves with a strong team that contains complimentary skills to their own.

They are not afraid of employing people with skills even greater than their own and, in fact, recognise that not to do that will ultimately hold them back in micromanagement, rather than being able to lead and pursue the big picture.

Jim Collins in *Good To Great* uses a metaphor for the venture, which is a bus – the leader is the driver and the staff are the passengers. He says that it's more important to have the right people on the bus than even to know where the bus is going at the outset. If you have the right people on the bus then, between you all, you will ultimately work out where the destination is and how to get there. By definition this requires an enormous leap of faith in recruiting fantastic people as a priority, even if you aren't quite sure of the role they will fill, since together you'll work it all out. I think this might work in larger ventures where incremental increases in staff numbers are relatively benign, but in a smaller enterprise employing, say, ten staff, it's simply not realistic to recruit a fantastic person and increase the workforce by 10% just because you think they are inspirational.

Having said that, exceptional people can get you exceptional results and you don't often find them applying for the role you've just advertised. So, if you come across truly exceptional people, wherever that may be, *then find a role for them* and they will help to drive your business. Just be careful of becoming over-enamoured with someone because you are personally attracted to them, rather than because they are genuinely brilliant, which can happen – especially with hot sales people who are naturally brilliant at creating empathy but in reality might be quite superficial.

Make recruitment choices slowly. In my experience, gut instinct can be wrong and you can spend a long time regretting quick decisions when it comes to people on your team.

Frankly, staffing is one of the areas that causes businesses the biggest headaches!

The fundamental problems with staffing are:

1. Staff have their own agenda, which is not generally or automatically aligned with that of the business.

2. Staff enjoy legal protection that was created in the industrial age when jobs were for life and it was the employer's role to take a patriarchal view of its employees. In today's fluid knowledge age, where jobs are often project based, it simply isn't realistic to offer such workplace continuity.

3. Many low-value production jobs have already been exported to low labour cost Asia, and those slightly up the scale have attracted cheaper labour nearer markets, which is by definition transitory. Business Process Outsourcing and the profusion of virtual assistants are more and more widespread.

4. Increasingly, jobs at all levels, even management, are being superseded by computers and robots (Moore's Law again!).

With so much cost and inflexibility in this area and so much change afoot, it is vital that leaders stay abreast of developments and continue to reappraise, redeploy and renew their staff and staffing arrangements, with a view to constantly increasing their efficiency.

There is no doubt that in a small business, where the leader's relationship with the team needs to be high trust in order to increase efficiency and reduce friction, the constant need to trim the team is one of the biggest challenges. If mishandled, it can be a disaster for the business in the short term; alternatively, if not faced, then it is an absolute long-term disaster as businesses become overburdened with cost and uncompetitive. Business owners need to ensure that they are hard but fair and that they stay close – but not too close – to their people.

Owners need to make sure that they measure the efficiency of the recruitment process, and that their people's goals are as closely aligned with the business's goals as possible. The best way of ensuring this is to involve them in the strategy formulation. In that way, they will feel a sense of ownership over the business's goals. If possible, actual ownership would be desirable through creating the greatest level of buy-in – literally. By this I don't mean gifting shares or share options, but rather some kind of actual buy-in where staff give cash in exchange for shares, as this is the best way of improving efficiency.

Getting this right in **YOUR business** is really key, especially when considering whether to reward results individually, by department or company-wide. It's a hard strategy to implement, especially if you've never done it before, but don't let inexperience stop you. If you're not sure where to begin, or even if it's right for your organisation (it almost always is), then get in touch. Simply email me at stephen.sacks@fundingnav.com and I can take you through the steps. Once you do it, you'll be amazed at how effective it is.

Sam Smith of broker FinnCap describes her ascendance as, *"not all plain sailing"*. In 2010, having invested £500k of her own earnings and bonuses into an MBO, Smith found herself with 48 hours to raise £2.5m to purchase the bulk of the remaining shares. Speaking at a business breakfast meeting, she said, *"Because of the split we initially made, we quickly ran out of that initial 50% to share around new employees, and there was 50% that could be used to drive the business faster if in the right hands. We managed to raise the money in 24 hours from the staff, which gave us a chance to create a really good, egalitarian culture."* Smith gives credit to the structure in facilitating the business's subsequent rapid growth. *"The day after the share raise, the atmosphere in the firm changed completely. Gone were the silos, politics and in-fighting that plague most businesses, replaced with a positive can-do attitude, where management became easier and increasingly unnecessary."*

Steve Olenski, writing in *Forbes*, says that hiring the right employees can make or break your business.

Employee recruitment is about managing stress, as you will constantly be judged on your selection, and you obviously cannot please everybody in your organisation.

The Six Rules to Hire the Right Employee for Your Business

1. Look for someone with a commitment to their career

A person committed to his or her career is the candidate you want to hire. You don't want to hire an employee who switches careers or jobs frequently, just to get a higher salary. If a candidate is not loyal to any company, hiring this person could certainly be a problem for your business.

Always check the candidate's previous job duration and, if he or she is switching jobs constantly, this is definitely not the right person.

2. Test for excellent learning and analytical skills

Try to use different methodologies to assess the learning and analytical skills of your candidates. Testing candidates might be tricky, but don't evaluate them merely on the basis of their resumé and their confidence, because a resumé can contain lies. Satish Bakhda from Rikvin.com believes that a candidate with confidence is great, but what you really want is a candidate that has the right skills and educational requirements.

3. Check compatibility

You want to find an employee that will fit in with your company's culture. Check whether the candidate has social skills to get along with others, especially with current employees and managers. Ask how he or she is managing current business clients to judge compatibility skills. Remember, willingness is one of the primary things a candidate must possess to work with you. And if a person cannot get along with his or her current clients or previous bosses, it's not such a great idea to hire that candidate.

4. Keep improving your hiring process

Whether you are hiring employees for a big organisation or looking for some potential candidates to build your start-up, the hiring process is the first and foremost factor you need to focus on. Make sure you follow these steps in your hiring process:

» Instead of asking magic bullet or irrelevant questions, you always need to focus on getting to know the capabilities, knowledge, skills, confidence, attitude and potential of the candidate.

» When you advertise job vacancies for your company, make sure that all the job requirements, such as responsibilities, education, experience, knowledge and skills, are clearly mentioned. This will help you in evaluating candidates and attracting applicants that fulfill all your requirements.

» It's also a good idea to involve other people in the evaluation process, since more opinions can lead to finding the right hire.

5. Don't forget to hire interns

Some may disagree, but this is one of the best ways to hire the right employee for your business. You'll discover all their strengths, weaknesses, skills, knowledge, attitudes, behaviour and confidence levels, and even get practical evidence of work. What else do you need to know?

You've already done the hard work in picking an intern, so why not hire from this potential pool when looking to fill permanent positions?

6. Get social with candidates

Asking personal questions won't get you anywhere and could be awkward and uncomfortable for both parties. Rather, you or your human resources team should be analysing candidates' presence on social media. This can be a great strategy, especially if you want to hire employees for tech businesses.

You'll be surprised what you can find out about a candidate by researching their social presence. Did you know that more than 90% of companies prefer to recruit through social media platforms such as Facebook, Twitter and LinkedIn?

If you look at the list of *Fortune 500 firms*, you'll see that 45% of these firms list job openings on social media.

Today, the team of most businesses extends way beyond the office (if there even is one), to a bevy of freelancers, outsourced contractors and virtual assistants that allow the enterprise the flexibility and low-cost base it needs to both survive and prosper. The challenges in aligning these external resources with the values and aims of the business, especially when they are so remote, are extreme, but the ultimate rewards are great. There are, of course, numerous tools at the modern leader's disposal, such as Skype and shared document apps.

Key Points

- » Stay close to the people in the business, but not too close.
- » Be prepared to act quickly to cut out negativity, as it's always destructive.
- » Keep improving your hiring processes.
- » Make full use of candidates' social media in assessing them.
- » Keep abreast of the level of efficiency you're achieving, and always strive to stay ahead of the curve by making rapid changes. Adopt new technology that helps facilitate quickly.
- » Allow your people a buy-in at both the strategy and equity level if at all possible, since the business's levels of efficiency

will be massively boosted. However, this doesn't mean create share option schemes, which can often do more to disincentivise rather than incentivise. If possible, get your guys to get some skin in the game.

» 80/20: make sure staff aren't wasting both your time and theirs by spending it simply moving information around or conducting never-ending internal meetings, rather than using it to create meaningful work of importance. *This includes you!*

4

Setting Your Flash Out

Setting your flash out' is the slang for what market traders do each morning when they set their stall up. In operating in this fundamental and original area of commerce, they have *two real advantages* over more complex businesses:

1. **They get to reinvent their strategy each day**, as each day the 'shop' has to be set up as new. This gives them a great opportunity to change their pricing and proposition according to lessons learnt the previous day and the current situation – for example, umbrellas at the front if it looks like rain. Also, if they arrive early enough, then there may be the opportunity to literally change their position in the market physically according to where they perceive greater customer flow to be. This is an enormous advantage compared to businesses that operate on a system of vertical ascension, where each development is consolidated and then built on again, and legacy issues persist in an ongoing erosion of the business's potential.

2. **They get real and relevant feedback from their punters in real time,** and they receive this qualitatively rather than as a load of numbers on a computer screen spreadsheet or in a power point presentation. Seeing what people are buying and why and, perhaps more importantly, what they are not buying and why, offers an immediate call to action. This is quite unlike the somewhat vanilla information that computers spew out that often does little to focus protagonists on the immediate job in hand and

create resolution strategies, but just leads to clever accounting as a means to hide the issue, instead of biting the bullet and dealing with it immediately.

All businesses in all sectors should think about adopting the market trader's strategies as far as they possibly can, because that is, after all, where the term 'marketing' comes from. It's no wonder that many ex market traders make such great business leaders, such as Tom Singh of *New Look* and *The Apprentice's* Lord Sugar. Time spent as a leader meeting with actual customers and gaining first-hand feedback from the coalface is of enormous value.

Trading ability is one of the most valuable skills anyone can possess in business.

When that skill is combined with an innate feel for the market and also a willingness to be proved wrong and to learn and get better, these are key success drivers to any business. The choice of product or service that the company will offer is the most fundamental decision that the entrepreneur will make. If that decision is wrong and not improved upon, then the venture is likely to be doomed to fail from the outset. In today's world, that initial decision needs to be constantly revisited because the market moves on so quickly. Fashion, technology and competition conspire to create an environment of accelerated product and service redundancy that we ignore at our peril.

Leaders can choose to spend their time in three basic fundamental activities:

1. Running today's business, which is where most people start, but if you want to develop and grow then spending time here will not be useful. It is, however, tough to move yourself back from the front line and trust others to do the fire fighting.

2. Improving today's business, which is definitely better than spending time running it, but you're still subject to being blindsided as focus remains inward.

3. Planning tomorrow's business, which is the toughest challenge for a business owner as it literally needs them to cut loose from the day-to-day and not consider incremental improvements, but an entirely different business. The more time invested here, the better the enterprise's long-term prospects for building real equity and value over time. Whilst not trying to blow my own trumpet too much, this is definitely an area where external consultants can make a real difference. They can challenge and task the business owner with this job, as he or she will inevitably find themselves attracted to the much more immediate issues of the current trading environment. So staying in this space is tough.

Businesses need to be planning for product and service redundancy in shorter and shorter time frames than ever before. They need to be milking their cash cows to subsidise their new innovations, knowing that there will be a high level of failure, because it's all about learning and using that learning to improve in the short and medium term, and then developing the next big thing. But even the next big thing will only have limited legs, so the process needs to be circular and ongoing.

A well-known company that demonstrates the increasing speed of reinvention required to succeed today, rather than historically, is Nokia, a company founded by Fredrik Idestam in 1865 as a pulp paper mill in the south west of Finland, which at the time was part of Russia. Over the next century, the business developed, sometimes through bankruptcy and consolidation, into a conglomerate with interests in many industries, producing at various times paper products, car and bicycle tyres, footwear (including rubber boots), communications cables, televisions and other consumer electronics, personal computers, electricity generation machinery, robotics, capacitors, military technology and equipment (such as the SANLA M/90 device and the M61 gas mask for the Finnish Army), plastics, aluminium and chemicals.

In the 1970s and 1980s, Nokia developed the Sanomalaitejärjestelmä ('*Message device system*'), a digital, portable and encrypted text-based communications device for the Finnish Defence Forces.

Nokia was a key developer of GSM (2G) (*Global System for Mobile Communications*), the second-generation mobile technology that could carry data as well as voice traffic. NMT (*Nordic Mobile Telephony*), the world's first mobile telephony standard to allow international roaming, provided expertise for Nokia in developing GSM, which was adopted in 1987 as the new European standard for digital mobile technology.

Nokia delivered its first GSM network to Finnish operator Radiolinja in 1989. The world's first commercial GSM call was made on 1 July 1991 in Helsinki, over a Nokia-supplied network. The by-then Prime Minister of Finland, Harri Holkeri, used a prototype Nokia GSM phone. In 1992, the first GSM phone, the Nokia 1011, was launched.

GSM's high-quality voice calls, easy international roaming and support for new services like text messaging (Short Message Service) laid the foundations for a worldwide boom in mobile phone use. GSM came to dominate mobile telephony in the 1990s, by mid 2008 accounting for about three billion subscribers, with more than 700 mobile operators across 218 countries and territories. Connections were growing at the rate of 15 per second, or 1.3 million per day.

Nokia launched the Nokia 3310 in 2000. It has become one of the most popular devices of all time. The Nokia 1100 handset launched in 2003, shipped over 200 million units, is the best-selling mobile phone ever, the world's top-selling consumer electronics product, and contributed to the company's rise in developing markets.

The Nokia ring tone was ubiquitous and annoying for a long time, and people were obsessed with playing the somewhat irritating signature game of '*Snakes*'. Almost unbeatable from 2000 for nearly a decade, Nokia posted record growth in both revenue and earnings annually. Even Apple's launch of the original iPhone in 2007 didn't really dent their sales, and Nokia continued the momentum until the launch of Apple's iPhone 3G in 2008. Apple's year-on-year market share doubled by the end of that year, and the market share of iPhone OS (now known as iOS) pulled ahead of Windows Mobile, although Nokia retained a 40.8% share by Q4 (4th quarter) 2008; nevertheless, it did see a decline of over 10% from Q4 2007, replaced by Apple's increasing share.

The rest is history. Like its business phone rival Blackberry, Nokia was basically destroyed by the growth of Apple's iPhone and their main competitors, the manufacturers of android devices such as Samsung. On 2 September 2013, Microsoft announced that it would acquire Nokia's mobile device business in a deal worth $4.25bn, which is a large amount of money until you consider that Apple is now the most valuable company in the world, with a value of over $650bn, or about 150 times the value of Nokia then. It has in fact been forecast to become the world's first trillion-dollar business.

So, a business that stayed abreast of change for over 100 years and moved into and dominated a category that defined an age in the early 2000s became irrelevant within just five years, because it was completely overhauled by a more nimble and aggressive competitor – a competitor that totally got the market dynamics, whilst Nokia evidently did not. So, even a century track record is irrelevant in guiding buyer demand.

If Nokia had been more sensitive to the market, they may well have been able to better predict the changes required and, given their enormous resources, have employed sufficient power to beat Apple at their own game – or else bought the upstart company, which itself was virtually bankrupt in 1996 just before Steve Jobs rejoined. But they didn't!

Good marketing means that the requirement to sell declines.

Anyone visiting an Apple Store, for example, will not be aggressively targeted by sales people. There is no need for the company to do that since its customers are quite prepared to camp out overnight in anticipation of being amongst the first to receive the newest iteration of a device. Products are tangible and patentable, and are therefore easier to engineer with a USP, as Apple does. Services, however, are neither tangible nor generally patentable, and therefore present the business owner with a more complex marketing problem.

Ultimately, services are about reputation, results and relationships. The absolute, if somewhat controversial, master of services marketing was Bernie Madoff. Regrettably, Bernie was unavailable for interview at the time of writing, given that he is currently serving 150 years in a Federal Correctional Institution in Butner Medium, North Carolina, for running the biggest Ponzi scheme ever uncovered. (Note the word 'uncovered' as the FBI claim that there are potentially much larger horrors lurking.)

If you can, try to see the 2017 film *The Wizard of Lies*, which sees Robert De Niro take on the role of Madoff. Not that it's such a great movie in all honesty, but it is an instructional look at Bernie's marketing strategy. Bernie never really prospected for sales himself, at least not outwardly. He relied on his existing clients to do that for him by referral. He would remain aloof from most people by making it difficult for new clients to contact him and work with him. By playing hard to get (a dating strategy used to great effect by teen girls) and developing a legend (which in his case was entirely fabricated), he managed to stimulate a huge demand for his services, which were to provide the illusion of large returns on fake investments. Highly successful business people, who frankly should have known better, would pursue him relentlessly to invest because of the stories they'd heard from those they trusted who had been conned into believing the hype. Ultimately, Madoff accepted sums in excess of $50bn from these greedy fools, without the requirement to employ high-pressure, boiler-room-type tactics. He simply created a marketing story that was so compulsive it was never really tested until it finally collapsed. One wonders how he may be profiting right now through creating markets from within Butner Medium Federal Correctional Institution.

So, try to analyse how you spend your time in running today's business, improving today's business and imagining tomorrow's business, and gradually move yourself out of today into tomorrow.

Always be trialling new marketing ideas, including the competition's.

Key Points

» Don't rest on your laurels or believe your own hype – ever (however great your mum thinks you are...)!

» Watch the competition closely and don't be afraid to steal their ideas to trial.

» Be prepared to totally reinvent your business over a cycle of every seven years.

» 80/20: only spend about 20% of your time working on today's business. Split the other 80% between improving today's business and creating tomorrow's business.

» Use pragmatic and external sounding boards (not your mum) to help create and test new ideas and strategies, before committing to trialling them commercially.

» Stay available but not overly accessible to your market to try to create a sense of exclusivity, as that will add an allure and a premium to your offer.

» And don't get involved in a Ponzi scheme, whatever you do!

5

Fill Your Funnel & Fix the Leaks

Sales is basically a three-stage process:

1. Prospecting.
2. Qualifying.
3. Closing.

It's essentially a numbers game and you really *must know your numbers* in order to succeed at it.

The two most important numbers fundamental to it are:

1. Lifetime customer value.
2. Cost of customer acquisition.

Since acquiring customers is generally a costly exercise, the easiest and cheapest way to improve sales is to increase the lifetime customer value of existing customers by upselling and cross-selling, as well as having a strategy of reconnecting with lapsed or resting customers.

At some point, however, most businesses will need to recruit new customers, even if they just want to stand still to counter natural leakage. Again, this is a numbers-driven exercise where you aim to fill the sales funnel with as many prospects as possible. Then, through a process of qualification, you whittle this number down to qualified leads and try to close as many of them as possible.

Let's go back to the example of Bernie Madoff, as I can say more or less what I like with impunity about Bernie and his methods, since this book will be long forgotten by the time of his theoretical release. Let's say that each month he received an average of ten referrals of hot leads looking to invest in his scheme at a stated 10% return per month. Bernie probably qualified them by considering how much they wanted to invest and how diligent they were. So, for example, a billionaire's widow looking for a home for multi hundreds of millions would probably be a preferential lead to a fund manager looking to trial a few million, as the former seems to present significantly greater returns than the fund manager, with much less risk of discovery. Bernie would probably have met personally with the widow initially, and then regularly afterwards in order to get her to increase her investments. However, he may well have rejected the latter entirely, who would then have reinforced Bernie's myth of inaccessibility.

So, if you want to sell like Madoff, you need to first *identify* who your ideal customers are and, in most cases, they most probably look like your current best customers. You then need to work out *where they hang out,* either literally (the golf club in Bernie's case), or maybe electronically – LinkedIn or Facebook etc. Having fielded them marketing messages that we discussed in the previous section, you will receive enquiries. These prospects are now leads since they actively want to be sold to. Qualifying the lead is key to not wasting resources, which will only increase the cost of customer acquisition. So before committing to expensive closing strategies like face-to-face meetings, you really need to sort the wheat from the tyre kickers.

The worldwide web has facilitated a huge move on for the sales and marketing industry. It is now possible to qualify leads better than ever before and for very niche small businesses to offer themselves to a narrow niche internationally. Also, the measurability and immediacy offer the marketer unprecedented levels of control over their budget spend. The web also, however, represents the single largest inefficiency in businesses, as resources are wasted on ill-thought-out and often worthless activities such as being omnipresent on social media, which feels proactive but may in reality be a complete dead end.

The internet has certainly given more options than ever before, but the time available to us all remains constant and the internet provides numerous distractions for wasting that time. It's also a bit of a zero-sum game since everyone is competing for the same customers' pixels and therefore often ignoring more traditional methods of filling the sales funnel, such as exhibitions and press advertising etc. Ongoing trial and error across various media and marketing strategies is absolutely vital, even if – or rather especially when – the current methods are working really well.

The sales funnel is often presented as a chart that indicates a company's current leads, prospects and opportunities. It is divided into several distinct stages. While the number and name of each stage might vary by company and sales process, each funnel ideally begins with a very large pool of potential customers and ends with a lesser number of closed sales.

The sales funnel earns its name from the natural manner by which the initial pool of leads is filtered down through a process that identifies the most promising potential customers – they're the ones towards whom marketing and sales will direct most of their resources. The qualification procedures determining which customers are most interested, or best fit buyer criteria, can help identify your sales team's best chances for a closed deal from a pool of leads that might be otherwise too numerous to address. Therefore, the *procedures underlying the sales funnel* can improve the efficiency of your sales process and also your sales and marketing ROI.

It's almost a trope that marketing and sales departments have ingrained, mutual dissatisfaction. Marketing attempts to build brand awareness, create value among prospects, and expand the initial, top-of-the-funnel pool of leads. Sales, on the other hand, doesn't want to waste time with unqualified leads. Coordination between the departments for the vetting process for leads can reduce frustration between the teams and ensure marketing's efforts produce the best leads sales can handle.

Understanding the **six basic stages** of the sales funnel can help you build an effective lead qualification process, determine the optimal hand-off point from marketing to sales, reduce friction between teams and improve overall ROI. For businesses nearing the point where a large number of leads are going unaddressed, this might make the difference between closing more deals and accepting a limit to your company's performance.

The Six Basic Stages of the Sales Funnel

1. Prospect

A prospect is *someone for whom contact information is available to your company*. In terms of digital marketing, a lead may be someone who simply visited your website. Lead generation efforts, particularly inbound marketing, which involves producing interesting, shareable content relevant to potential customers, can result in a high quantity of website traffic. Many of these visitors can be induced to yield their contact details in exchange for a gated asset, like an ebook, a video, a white paper, and so on.

Once they've submitted their contact details, the lead can transition from an unqualified prospect – identifiable only through IP address – to a qualified lead. In these terms, anyone can become a prospect, and the exit criteria of qualification is simple. However, as many online visitors are reluctant to divulge their contact details, there can be significant drop off or 'leakage' from this top-of-the-funnel stage.

2. Qualified Lead

A lead becomes qualified after they have *willingly identified themselves to the company*. At this point, their website activity can be tracked, and having likely provided their email address, they can be recipients of email marketing outreach. Their activity relating to your emails can also be tracked. In this way, you can determine which website pages they visit, which links they click, what other assets they download, whether they look at your pricing page and how long they linger. Regarding your emails, you can see which ones they open, how long it took them to open it after receipt, and which links or attachments they open. (Meanwhile, the customer experience on your website can be curated through custom landing pages with content tailored to specific links – this is a form of lead nurturing.)

Tracking visitors' website and email activity allows for more precise lead qualification as well as more accurate website metrics, like traffic sources by segment or top pages for conversions, and email metrics, like open-rates and click-through rates. Certain online actions or traits can be weighted for lead-scoring purposes – the number of visits to a pricing page, the number of emails opened or the types of links clicked, even the type of email address. Therefore, the more comprehensive your knowledge of the lead, the more accurate their lead score and the likelier a higher-scoring lead will progress to the sales team. Evidently, the exit criteria for leads – to become a **Marketing Qualified Lead** – is to attain a score reaching the threshold for transferral to the sales team.

3. Marketing Qualified Lead

A Marketing Qualified Lead (MQL) is a lead that has *ranked highly in the marketing and sales teams' jointly-developed lead-scoring model.* This model, which is regularly reviewed and updated, assigns scores to lead traits and behaviour that indicate the lead's buying potential. Leads are qualified on explicit criteria, such as job title, company, number of employees and location, implicit criteria like visited pages or downloaded assets, and timeline and negative criteria, which is anything that has a negative correlation with a closed deal. The sum of the lead score elements should indicate whether the qualified lead is ready for contact from a salesperson, or requires further lead nurturing; this threshold is also determined through cooperation between the two departments.

Qualified leads fall generally within a four-quadrant matrix measured by fitness and interest. A 'fit' lead possesses explicit criteria similar to your hypothetical ideal customer. An 'interested' lead demonstrates behaviour along the same lines. Charted against two axes, with fitness and interest assigned to either axis, an MQL will fall in the upper right quadrant. The exit criteria for an MQL to become a 'Sales Accepted Lead' is, of course, acceptance by the sales department. Much of the process described to this point can be automated by workflows with marketing automation software.

4. Sales Accepted Lead

There is overlap between an MQL and a Sales Accepted Lead (SAL), as there is often disagreement over the quality of leads transferred from marketing to sales. The lead-scoring model corresponds with past buyer behaviour – salespeople can recognise buyer attributes that may be hard to quantify. Sales-specified criteria adds a filter to the MQLs that prioritises leads according to your sales team's instincts.

Facing more qualified leads than your sales team can handle is a good problem to have. The SAL stage becomes especially relevant when dealing with an excess of MQLs, when a sales agent's time on lesser-qualified leads comes at the expense of an easier or higher-performing sale. The SAL stage may apply a filter based on BANT criteria (Budget, Authority, Needs, Timeline) or more intangible factors like goals and priorities. An SAL is considered highly suitable for follow-up contact and moves further along the funnel.

5. Sales Qualified Lead/Opportunity

A Sales Qualified Lead (SQL) has gone through *several rounds of internal vetting and is ready for contact by a salesperson.* This contact will likely occur over the medium your salesperson feels is best. Traditionally, at this stage, the salesperson will manage a product demonstration and preliminary pricing. Today, this largely depends on the industry and the product. For certain services, like most kinds of software-as-a-service and most vendors therein, product demos are available as a gated asset. This means the potential customer can try out the product and determine their own interest before they ever reach the MQL stage.

However, in many cases still, the SQL stage is when a salesperson guides a demo, allays a customer's potential concerns, and clearly articulates the product's benefits, the on-boarding process (if applicable), post-purchase support, preliminary pricing and any other factors related to the deal (NDA as well, if applicable).

When you hear the phrase 'sales pipeline', it typically relates to the qualification and sales process in the SAL/SQL stages. Of course, if the sales process goes well, it results in a closed deal – at which point the lead proceeds to the last stage of the funnel.

6. Customer

Congratulations! You closed the deal. But the job's not done. Built into your sales process should also be the delivery and follow-up – ensuring that once the proverbial ink on the contract is dry, the customer is still happy. Salespeople know that effective follow-up can result in new connections and new leads, either within the customer's company or outside it, if not immediately then possibly in the future. In addition, the customer should be reminded of what support options are available for the product or service they purchased. This stage is the last in the marketing and sales funnel, and in your sales automation software, the deal would be closed as 'won'. Good job!

The marketing and sales funnel provides structure to the sales process – not to mention, when visualised, offering a snapshot of existing prospects, leads and opportunities. Clearly defined sales funnel stages with entrance and exit criteria ensure due diligence in promotion of the best qualified leads, and contribute data that allows you to study and refine the process further, with metrics such as visitor-to-lead rate, percentage of Sales Accepted Leads, and opportunity-to-customer-conversion rate.

Routinely analysing the procedures underlying your sales funnel in response to bottlenecks, leaks or changing conditions allows you to improve upon ingrained practices, precisely direct your marketing and sales resources and increase your overall ROI.

We have had great success introducing prospecting campaigns that utilise LinkedIn, Facebook (especially retargeting), affiliates, national press, exhibitions and conferences, catalogues and probably still the number one growth driver even now – TV.

LinkedIn is great for B2B. It offers the marketer the most direct way to select and communicate with their target by geography, industry, company size and job title, as well as providing a career history of the target and a ton of other information that you can use to tailor your approach. There are great businesses out there providing innovative LinkedIn based solutions that we can put you in touch with.

Similarly, Facebook provides unprecedented granularity to the marketer to reach consumers with ultra-targeted messages. Facebook is credited to a large extent with the recent political turmoil across the world as a result of Donald Trump's victory in the 2016 presidential elections and the UK's historic decision to Brexit. Trump famously achieved success at a fraction of the cost of Clinton's failure and much of this was due to his mastery of social media, specifically Facebook. Via this platform, his team were able to send quite specific messages to the Obama disenfranchised, explaining how they would 'make America great again' relative to a local issue such as the automotive industry in Detroit or agriculture in Idaho. Similarly, the UK Brexit campaign targeted fishermen in Grimsby with messages about the EU fisheries policy, and how the UK would take back control of the North Sea post Brexit. Concurrently, they targeted metal bashers in the Midlands with messages of how, post Brexit, the UK would be able to limit imports of industrial materials and protect their jobs.

The undisputed winner of both competitions was, of course, Facebook, which made hundreds of millions in advertising revenues.

Facebook also offers advertisers the opportunity to retarget its users following their visit to relevant websites. This gives potential buyers the impression that your company is advertising everywhere for very little budget, as the targeting is extremely narrow and focused. It's why relevant messages follow you round the internet.

Affiliate marketing offers the huge bonus that its costs are normally totally sales related rather than lead or click related. However, the most successful affiliate sites are discount or voucher-code based, and sometimes these only serve to erode the margin on sales, as potential full-price customers are relegated to discount buyers, so beware! The way this works is that many consumers are conditioned to search for discount codes when in the checkout process. Try to avoid this at all costs!

Mass-market media, such as press and TV, can be accessed nowadays for a surprisingly reasonable cost and gives consumers a massively inflated view of your brand. The fragmentation that has occurred in mass media and improvements in technology have also enabled the ability to target very specific consumer groups and measure and track the results, which is absolutely key if you have limited budget. Did you know, for example, that Sky boxes can field entirely different ads in the same programme to neighbouring houses, depending on the advertiser's requirements and the viewer's profile?

Exhibitions and conferences offer you a great opportunity, whether B2B or B2C, to meet your potential customers direct and face-to-face, like the example of the market stall holder given earlier. These are therefore massively valuable, not just as a marketing strategy, but as a research strategy too.

Ultimately, however, as the old adage goes, *people buy from people.* Whether you employ telesales, field sales or even bots, you need to think very carefully about the customer journey and the customer experience. Use of mystery shoppers and online testers, and also shopping your competitors, are all key strategies for ensuring that you're able to maximise on your lead-generation investment by maximising your close rate.

Sales people often have poor reputations as they are synonymous with high-pressure methodologies or badly targeted approaches. If, however, the marketing campaign has done its job right then the sales people should be in receipt of a growing stream of people to speak to who have a problem that they need to spend time understanding, before coming back with a solution. Good sales guys listen and then offer the customer a solution to their problem in an honest and straightforward way. They build trust through not being pushy or self-serving, and therefore increase not only the chances of conversion, but also the customer's lifetime value and the opportunity of a referral, which is generally the best way to fill the funnel.

There are two distinctly different types of sales person – hunter and farmer. Businesses should be very careful to ensure that roles are properly specified and that the right people are put into the right roles. Hunters are key at the outset of a business as they will build and replicate new customers. Farmers are the follow-up, but they are actually where most of the money is earned through building long-term and mutually beneficial relationships. Putting farmers into hunting roles will result in very low levels of new business since they are more coy than hunters. Putting hunters into farming roles will result in low repeat business and high levels of staff turnover, since hunting is a way of life and these guys, if they are good, will already have their next job lined up even as they accept the current job. Similarly, remuneration schemes need to differ for each role. Hunters need to be rewarded for closing new deals specifically and to be targeted on those, and farmers for year on year growth within their specific accounts.

Practising effective sales strategies can be seen as a bit old fashioned now, as so many of the ideas emanate from trainers such as Dale Carnegie 100 years ago, but just because they are tried doesn't mean that they shouldn't be trusted.

Good sales people have to be effective at:

» **Empathising** – understanding what the customer wants and why.

» **Opportunism** – looking at every scenario as a potential sale.

» **Administration** – following up when follow-up is required.

» **Robustness** – sales isn't for precious snowflakes. The declining sales funnel (i.e. the majority of leads will not convert) means that handling rejection and coming back again and again and again are undoubtedly the top salesperson's key qualities.

New customer acquisition, as already discussed, is basically a numbers game, so…

Before setting up a campaign you must know the average lifetime value of a customer: that is **net revenue annually** *multiplied* by the **average number of years customers stay with your organisation.**

So, for the sake of an example, let's say that the average customer relationship lasts for three years and the average customer's contribution to gross profit annually is £4k. Therefore, the average lifetime value of a customer is £12k.

Having worked that out, you now need to work out how much you are prepared to pay for a new customer. Obviously the answer must be less than £12k if you want to stay in business in the long term, but how much less really depends on how much cash you have, what the competition spends, how quickly you want to grow and your gross margin and overheads. Let's say, in our example, that you are prepared to spend 75% of the first year's revenue or £3k per customer on acquisition, and let's say that you want to attract 100 new customers this year. Therefore, the total budget we can allocate to this activity is £300k.

Now we need to know how many stages are in our sales funnel and what the conversion is at each stage. So, imagine that our example business attracts prospects by press advertising, followed by sending out catalogues. It then arranges appointments in customers' homes to sell to them. If sales guys convert a third of the customers they visit and catalogues generate 10% of appointments, we can calculate that we will need the following to generate 100 new customers:

> 3000 catalogues

> 300 meetings

Assuming a response rate in media of 0.1% (yes, typically it really can be as low as that) of readers who order catalogues, then we will need to reach three million of them initially.

> The £300k budget can then be allocated accordingly.

> Those 300 meetings can probably be managed by one sales guy with a budget of £60k, to include bonus and expenses.

> The cost of 3000 catalogues plus despatch will cost say £40k.

> A response centre handling the prospect leads, sending out the catalogues and making sales appointments is probably £100k.

➤ That leaves about £100k to generate the creative campaign and pay for the media that will reach three million readers.

Obviously one needs to tweak and experiment with all the stages in order to get the biggest bang for each buck, as every marginal improvement in performance will result in more customers for less cost.

So, given that in our example company a new customer costs £3k to acquire on average but will produce £12k in revenue over three years, you can see that even marginal improvements in acquisition of 20%, down to say £2.4k to acquire or a £600 saving, pale into insignificance with the opportunity to efficiently farm what you already have and increase the average annual spend by say 10%, and the average length of time a customer stays by 10%. These two changes will compound to increase the customer value by a total of £2.5k, which is three times the gain from more efficient acquisition. Therefore, you might choose to target your farmers with achieving both these goals and put £1k per existing customer into retention, since it will produce an ROI of 2.5 as against making marginal gains in acquisition efficiency.

As can be seen from these examples, after working out their numbers and honing their sales techniques to maximise return, ambitious businesses should spend as much as they can afford on sales and marketing. Certainly, they should aim to spend at levels that make the competition vomit. This is not a trite remark but merely an observation that most budgeting is set based on a finite set of revenue numbers for a year. However, provided you are in a position to quickly scale your delivery and you get your sales and marketing numbers right, then you should absolutely NOT limit your sales and marketing spend finitely but rather by return on investment. Sales and marketing is often expressed by businesses as a percentage of revenue of say 5%, which makes it seem like a drag. A good strategy from this position might be to reduce this cost by 1% to 4%, which should go straight to the bottom line. This simplistic thinking is arse upwards and conveniently ignores where the sales came from in the first place.

So, rather than state that you have a 5% cost, turn it around so that you earn £20 for every £4 you spend. Now spending less doesn't seem so attractive, does it? Imagine if, rather than spending £4, you spent £8 – how could that translate into £40 of sales? That's the question that you and your team should really be addressing!

Please refer to the equation of business section in the resources available to you at www.fundingnav.com to see the aggregate impact of making many small improvements to your numbers. I *guarantee* that you will be absolutely amazed at the enormous overall impact you can make on your bottom line profits by implementing small improvements across a series of measurables concurrently.

Key Points

» Know your numbers.

» Consider sales and marketing as an investment rather than a cost.

» Hone your approach to improve your numbers.

» Always be testing and always be experimenting.

» Think about your customers' experience.

» Try your competitors' customer experience and don't be afraid to borrow some of their best ideas.

» Always be making ongoing improvements to the efficiency of your sales pipeline.

» Spend so much on marketing that it makes your competitors vomit (no, really vomit). The question should be, once you have established your CPA and LCV, not how little but how much can I spend on this! So many companies just don't get it. Think of it like this: if you knew for sure that for every £10 you spent you could definitely receive a £20 return immediately, then how many lots of £10 would you spend? The answer should be: as many as possible. You certainly wouldn't want to sell yourself short here, would you?

6

The Easiest Money You'll Ever Make

If there's one business that's unlike most others because the key to success is less about sales and marketing and more about purchasing, then it's property. Property sales are generally highly commoditised, especially now in the internet age when buyers can compare the whole market from the comfort of their browser. If you attend a property networking event, you'll find that there is little concern about sales. Mostly, attendees are interested in two subjects: how to finance and buying at a discount to the market. We'll discuss finance in a subsequent chapter but it's instructive to look at the way success is gained in this market, and then to extrapolate this across all other markets.

Property investors are always looking for off-market opportunities that have motivated sellers standing behind them, because in their world that is where most of the margin of opportunity is. Given the piecemeal and lumpy nature of property, each transaction is negotiated separately, and much care goes into understanding the seller's needs and motivation, thus creating an opportunity to obtain a price advantage from them. When you are working with deals at this price level (hundreds of thousands or even millions), it is naturally worthwhile to do your homework and befriend the seller. You want to find out their motivation for selling and make yourself the most attractive buyer because of empathy or speed, then use this to give yourself a pricing advantage. Now, in the more regular world where individual transactions are a fraction of those in property, this is often forgotten, which is shocking because in aggregate all these costs are similarly huge.

In this more regular world of purchasing goods and services for resale by commercial businesses, we often get too comfortable with our supplier relationships. Therefore, deals that may have been competitive at the outset are sometimes not revisited, and deteriorate in relative competitiveness over time. We can get caught up in the general day-to-day stuff and we overlook probably the greatest opportunity we have to make a pretty much instantaneous improvement to our gross margin and bottom line profit – which is to renegotiate our input costs.

Negotiation is undoubtedly the quickest money you'll ever make. Even a two-minute phone call can result in thousands of pounds of additional profit over time. As in property, some homework on the seller's motivation and structure is pretty key because you will need to sell yourself to them as an ideal solution to their current issues. This is why buying a car is best done on the last day of the month or quarter, as the salesman, desperate to make his bonus for flogging just one more unit, will likely chuck in his children to secure a deal, never mind just a regular discount at that time.

Negotiation is defined as a discussion among individuals to reach a conclusion acceptable to one and all. It is a process whereby people, rather than fighting among themselves, sit together, evaluate the pros and cons, and then come out with an alternative that would provide a win win situation for all.

For example, Sam wanted to purchase a mobile handset. He tried his level best to buy it at the lowest possible rate, and the shopkeeper ensured that he could earn his profits as well. Thus, the negotiation benefited Sam, who didn't have to shell out loads of money, and the shopkeeper was also satisfied because he earned some profits.

Negotiation helps in reducing conflicts and disputes among each other. It is essential in every walk of life for peaceful and stress-free living.

The Four Models of Negotiation

1. Win Win Model

In this model, each and *every individual involved* in the negotiation wins. Nobody loses and everyone benefits. This is the most accepted model of negotiation.

Let's understand it with the help of an example:

Daniel wanted to buy a laptop but it was an expensive model. He went to the outlet and negotiated with the shopkeeper to lower the price. Initially the shopkeeper was reluctant but, after several rounds of discussions and persuasion, he quoted a price best suited to him as well as to Daniel. Daniel was extremely satisfied as he could now purchase the laptop without burning a hole in his pocket. The negotiation also benefited the store owner as he could earn his profits, plus he gained a loyal customer who would shop with him again in future too.

2. Win Lose Model

In this model, *one party wins and the other party loses.* After several rounds of discussions and negotiations, with this model one party benefits while the other remains dissatisfied.

Please refer to the above example once again, where Daniel wanted to buy a laptop. In this example, both Daniel and the store owner benefited from the deal. Let's suppose Daniel could not even afford the price quoted by the store owner and requested him to lower it further. If the store owner did further lower the price, he would not be able to earn his profits but Daniel would be very happy. Thus, after the negotiation, Daniel would be satisfied but the shopkeeper wouldn't. In a win lose model, both parties aren't satisfied. Only one of them walks away with the benefit.

3. Lose Lose Model

As the name suggests, in this model, the outcome of negotiation is *zero. No party is benefited out of this model.*

Had Daniel not purchased the laptop after several rounds of negotiation, neither he nor the store owner would have got anything out of the deal. Daniel would leave empty handed and the store owner would obviously earn nothing.

In this model, generally neither party is willing to accept the other's views, and both are reluctant to compromise.

4. RADPAC Model of Negotiation

The RADPAC Model of Negotiation is widely used in companies. It will definitely help you to systemise a strategy like this in your business. **Predictably, every letter in this model signifies something:**

R – Rapport

A – Analysis

D – Debate

P – Propose

A – Agreement

C – Close

R – **Rapport:** as the name suggests, this signifies the relationship between parties involved in negotiation. They should ideally be comfortable with each other and share a good rapport.

A – **Analysis:** one party must understand the second party well. It is important that the individuals understand each other's needs and interests. The shopkeeper must understand the customer's needs and pocket; in the same way, the customer mustn't ignore the shopkeeper's profits. People must listen to each other attentively.

D – **Debate:** nothing can be achieved without discussions. This round includes discussing issues among the parties involved in negotiation. The pros and cons of an idea are evaluated here. People debate with each other and each one tries to convince the other. No one must lose their temper in this round, but should remain calm and composed.

P – **Propose:** each individual proposes their best idea in this round, trying their hardest to come up with the optimum possible idea and to reach a conclusion acceptable to all.

A – **Agreement:** individuals come to a conclusion at this stage and agree to the best possible alternative.

C – Close: the negotiation is complete and individuals return satisfied.

Obviously getting at least two, and hopefully even three, quotes for everything will help you achieve a highly competitive price and a strong negotiating position. You should therefore make this a standard operating requirement, regardless of how attractive an initial quote seems and despite the fact that the salesman needs you to sign on the dotted line that day.

Beware the loading for loyalty! Nowadays, a lot of companies use the power of the internet and the discomfort and perceived inconvenience of change as a strategy to increase prices to their most loyal customers, as counter-intuitive as that sounds. Examples of this are stationery companies using algorithms that begin by quoting very low prices for repeatable commodities, such as paper, and then gradually increase the price to you with every new order. They then decrease it again if you slow or stop ordering. Many car insurers also operate like this. The aggregating insurance websites are generally linked to the insurers in any event, and most of the insurers that are on these sites purporting to be independent brands are all part of the same business too. Nine times out of ten, prices on renewal are substantially higher than those they quote for new customers, because they rely on the inertia and trust of customers and are prepared to lose a few strays along the way.

Negotiation skills are hugely valuable but, rather like with boxing, you have to be careful to always vary your initial approach.

Otherwise your regular suppliers will simply start playing the same game as you, and you'll find yourself side-lined. This is like in the souk, where sellers factor in a discount because both parties know how the game goes. It effectively becomes a zero-sum game in this case. It may be that sometimes you should go for price, sometimes for ancillaries such as delivery, and sometimes for payment terms. Obviously it is *absolutely key* that your supplier is able to make a profit because, if they fail, then ultimately that could have a negative outcome for you too i.e. lose lose. So you should work together with the supplier to understand their business dynamics, rather like in the example of the car salesman on page 68. The salesman is probably ultimately driven by the car manufacturers, who often price in retrospective discounts for volume with their dealer network. It might be that you can also use a referral, which you may make in the normal course of events in any case, as a bargaining chip to bring down the cost.

Of course, this attitude doesn't just apply to your core proposition purchase, but actually to everything you buy; even small incidentals and grudge purchases such as utilities, or hidden purchases like credit card and bank commission and charges, as well as foreign exchange rates. Let's take a business that has, say, a million pounds of costs. If someone applies themselves for just half an hour a day for a year to taking 10% out of these, then they will have made the business an additional £100k profit for about 100 hours of time, which correlates to £1k per hour. So that's not bad paid work, is it? Again, check out the equation of business exercise at www.fundingnav.com to see the positive impact that can be achieved.

This is one of the main areas where Funding Nav succeeds: *slashing costs for its clients*. Often we get offered substantially lower costs than our clients across a broad range of products and services, such as forex, utilities, logistics etc, as we have much more volume aggregated across our client base than any trading business. Sometimes this is even from the clients' existing suppliers, who are suddenly exposed to increasing levels of external rigour. Please email me at stephen.sacks@fundingnav.com to get a cross quote or to sense-check any pricing that you've been quoted.

Remember, in life we don't get what we deserve, but what we negotiate.

Key points

» Never *ever* accept anyone's first price for anything. If you don't ask for a discount, then you won't get one.

» Take time to understand your supplier's motivation and pain points and, if possible, help them. But at the same time, help yourself too.

» Change your tactics every time to prevent game playing.

» Always get other competitive quotes before purchasing anything*.

» RADPAC.

Sometimes sellers become friends or were friends in the first place, and this can make the negotiation process difficult. I often encounter this situation with SME owners. In this case, you should still comparison shop and present your findings to your friendly supplier as a way to help them better understand the competitive market they are in. Hopefully, if they are a true friend, they will then take the initiative and offer you a price reduction unilaterally.

7

Keep the Market Short to Charge a Premium to the Market Price

---

Pricing is key to an enterprise's success.

There are many ways to set prices but ultimately only one way to sustain them. This is to ensure that the market has more demand for what you are selling than you are able to supply. Most businesses perceive that they sell commoditised products and are therefore forced to sell at the market price. Indeed, setting prices at similar levels to competitors is a typical pricing strategy. The fact is, though, that there are numerous examples of subjective values being applied to products or services, which in many ways are similar to other commoditised products that are forced to sell at the market price.

Here are some examples of products and services where customers are willing to pay a significant premium of at least 100 times, despite the market being full of much cheaper, viable alternatives subjectively no better or worse at the job in hand than the expensive option.

Rolex vs Quartz watches – Quartz watches are actually more accurate than Swiss mechanical chronographs, yet people pay a massive premium for the status of the Swiss chronograph.

George Clooney vs anyone of the other half a million US screen actors – as attractive as he is, George suits some people but not others and is objectively not the best actor in America, yet he claims a massive premium from producers of motion pictures that he deigns to appear in when compared to most other actors.

Bentley vs Hyundai – both will get you to your destination in a similar time, but the Hyundai will do it statistically more reliably than the Bentley and at a hugely lower cost.

Jimmy Choo vs Aldo – Jimmy Choos may cripple you, but you can wear Aldos all day long for a fraction of the cost of the more exotic footwear choice.

The only key differences between each of these examples is that:

» All the expensive alternatives are kept in purposeful short supply (thank god for that in George Clooney's case – it would certainly make the market tougher for all other men if there were multiple Georges).

» The makers of the expensive alternatives have made a conscious effort to position themselves at the premium end of their respective markets, and to ask their customers for a high price.

» All the expensive alternatives have an additional quality to the cheaper competitor and this is generally around attraction. The fact is that consumers are attracted to Bentleys, Rolexes, Jimmy Choos and George Clooney emotionally, and they make irrational economic decisions in selecting these.

A recent and hilarious example of how keeping the market short drives enormous demand was demonstrated by the owner of *The Shed* in Dulwich. Now, the owner of this particular shed was formerly employed writing fake restaurant reviews on *Trip Advisor* for £10 each in order to boost the ratings of restaurants he had never visited. He decided to make his shed London's number-one-rated restaurant in a fascinating experiment.

He set up a website and bought a phone for £10. He then made up some dishes based on moods and took soft focus pictures of fake dishes that were largely constructed using sponge, shaving foam and paint. One picture was a fried egg on his foot on a plate. On 5 May 2017, *Trip Advisor* accepted his listing and he started out in last position of the 18,149 restaurants listed in London. He then got some friends to post some fake reviews and, in a few short weeks, his shed was in the top

10,000 restaurants rated on the website. Then the phone started ringing and genuine potential clients attempted to book. He obviously refused all bookings, claiming to be fully booked for months. The combination of this lack of availability, lack of address and by-appointment-only proposition proved so alluring that in another few weeks, he was in the top 1,500 and soon after, by August, at number 156.

Then things started to really get out of hand as *The Shed* began to receive free samples from companies, job applications, an email from the council offering a deal on a new site in Bromley, and an offer from an Australian TV production company looking to feature *The Shed* in a series of inflight videos about the world's best eateries. By winter 2017, *The Shed* was at number 30 in London and people were actively looking for the place physically. One day, emails started literally streaming in from across the world and the website was getting 89,000 hits in a day. The reason was that on 1 November 2017, *The Shed* became London's top-rated website on *Trip Advisor*. But still not one genuine customer had been served. There were just 103 made-up reviews and a load of frustrated demand!

Since the phone was now getting in excess of 100 calls per day, they decided to actually try serving some meals. These were purchased from Iceland and served in *The Shed* and the garden in response to clients' moods. The first clients flew in from California – I kid you not!

The deception was then quickly uncovered and *The Shed* was delisted from *Trip Advisor*, but not before demonstrating the enormous power of combining positive feedback with a shortage of supply.

So, there you go: ensure you appear alluring and oversubscribed, and the rest is just detail. To be fair, at some point you will need the back-up to prove your credentials, but only after you are already flying high. It really is all about selling the sizzle and not the sausage!

The Four Classifications of Business

Now, made-up businesses are one thing, but there are only really four classifications of real businesses:

1. Successful lifestyle businesses

2. Unsuccessful lifestyle businesses

3. Successful larger growth businesses

4. Unsuccessful larger declining businesses

If the owner of a successful lifestyle business wants to, then she can become a successful growth business potentially. It is, however, unlikely that an unsuccessful lifestyle business can become a successful growth business without first becoming a successful lifestyle business. So, the key to success is to stay small longer than you need to, and really bootstrap your growth as far as possible. This is because necessity is the mother of invention: you will find more inventive ways of doing things, and you will soon begin to create a USP by necessity, since it is a way of growing profitability without growing resources or revenue. Only when you have nailed this – and I mean *really nailed this* – should you start to consider adding more capacity, as you will almost certainly experience a drop in profitability as you move from a successful lifestyle business to a growth business.

The reasons for this are multiple, but essentially there are three problems:

1. If you add another person doing what you are doing, then suddenly the premium you were charging over what you were selling may drop because you just doubled the supply – but maybe the demand didn't double.

2. Since you are most likely the best performer as you started the business, and now you need to spend part of your time managing someone else, it means you will have less time to engage with the front end of the business than before.

3. It is likely that there was a premium on what you were selling before because it came from you directly, i.e. direct from the source, whereas, if someone else is now delivering, then it's not the same and the premium may drop. This is especially true of service-based concepts.

So, think *carefully* before deciding on your ultimate goal. Nowadays it is perfectly possible to develop an amazing lifestyle business geared through technology, external associates and virtual assistants, where you can charge a real premium over the market because you can become the George Clooney of your industry. The move from there to becoming a successful growth business is strewn with obstacles and it's likely that your premium and profitability will drop in the short to medium term. You will also find that the other reason you probably went into business, which was autonomy, will diminish too, as suddenly you have staff issues to consider. Ultimately you may find yourself back on the corporate hamster wheel that you were trying to escape in the first place.

It is actually highly likely that you will struggle to expand until you hit the rather magic number of a team of 12*.

Honestly, pricing is at the core of lots of business issues that Funding Nav sees, and you need the balls to trial different pricing strategies until you find the optimum one for your business. However, this is so much easier when you are not on a treadmill with overbearing overheads or cash issues.

A typical example we saw recently was a company that was running at full capacity making vegetable snacks. It had a 30,000 square foot factory running 24/7, and yet it was losing money. When I saw them, they were seeking external capital to expand in order to become profitable.

Our advice was not to borrow to expand, but instead to change their pricing, and specifically to increase their prices by 10%, accepting that there would be a short-term drop in demand. This drop we recommended they fill with better quality customers attracted by the premium offer. We did ourselves out of the work of getting them funded because their plan to run faster and faster on the same hamster wheel wouldn't have worked in the long term. There was no reason for the business to take on additional long-term commitments, or a distracting fund-raising exercise in the short term, when the answer was staring them in the face.

Price increases can be trialled and can always be reduced again if demand dries up 100%, which is what companies always fear is going to happen. I have never seen this, however.

Please visit the resource section at www.fundingnav.com to complete the spreadsheet that shows how small improvements in your numbers, especially pricing, will have a disproportionately positive impact on your bottom line.

Key Points

» Get your proposition nailed before even considering expansion.

» Even then, consider carefully your motivation for being in business.

» Create a niche for your business, and market strongly to that niche in a way that takes you out of having to price in response to the rest of the market.

» Don't be a busy fool. If you have low overheads, you can afford to be picky about what you take on. Then, because you are less busy, you will be able to really improve the offer to the customer, as you will have freed up so much time by not doing all the low-margin stuff. You then begin to really justify the premium that you charge.

» Remember that, in order to charge a premium to the market price, you only need to have a shortage in supply in the specific thing that you are selling. So, given that you aren't selling to the whole market, find the part of the market that will pay and market to them only.

One of our partners has a really interesting piece of IP called red, blue, black. Basically, blue represents revenue-generating activities, black is management activities, and red is administration. Obviously, the key to success is to employ the maximum amount of blues with the optimum amount of reds and blacks in support. They have calculated and have evidence that the optimum number of staff for an SME is 12. It's like a soccer team including the manager, or an army platoon.

8

Know Your Numbers

Rather like piloting an aeroplane in conditions of poor visibility, running a business can sometimes be disorientating. The pilot fixes onto points that are either incorrect or irrelevant when there are really key issues to focus on that are being conveniently ignored. This can easily lead you off into conflicting directions. The fact is that we humans are often emotional rather than logical creatures. We choose to focus on the areas of least pain rather than of most pain, which is where we should be focused. So typically, good news is latched on to and celebrated, whilst bad news is ignored or swept under the carpet. This will inevitably prove disastrous: either timely decisions are not taken or else the wrong decisions are made according to the comfort zone of the director, rather than according to the pressing requirement of the business.

It is therefore key that there are objective and up-to-date figures available to guide the decisions made within the business, so that actions taken will be at least guided by proper numbers. It is also useful if there is an independent stakeholder in the business who can hold the leader's feet to the fire. This can be one of the most fractious but also rewarding reasons to engage an independent advisor like Funding Nav – not just so that the issues can be pointed out, but also so that fixes can be both suggested and actioned quickly before things get critical or just diverted in the wrong direction.

There are numerous objective and subjective measures that relate to a business's success and, whilst some are common to all businesses, such as the cash flow and profit, others can be quite specific, such as houses for sale on an exclusive basis for estate agents, or occupation levels at a hotel. However, the main categories to measure are pretty similar across all businesses and the availability of numbers should relate to relevance and ease of production. So, some numbers might be difficult or expensive to produce frequently (such as staff surveys, which are tricky to produce monthly and probably of more value when viewed either quarterly or annually, which is fine), but others really must be available monthly.

What Needs Measuring

Typically, *cash flow* is the most important measure of a business's short-term health and serves as a summary of all the other factors at play. So, all businesses need to be watching that like a hawk because running out of cash is normally pretty critical.

Then, of course, there's *profit* which, like all the other measures, should be shown relative to the previous year and also relative to forecast.

The *sales and marketing* numbers obviously are key feeders into profit. These really need to be broken down as far as possible so that the sales pipeline can be analysed as well as the return on investment in both new and current sales, plus measures such as customer retention, sales per customer, sales per campaign, sales per agent or salesperson and, of course, margin on all these numbers too, if possible.

Then, *production and delivery* – so things like lead time and ancillary costs should be measured. And one measure that is often ignored (except in businesses that have very definite supply caps like hotels and airlines) is the measurement of spare capacity that can throw off a calculation of missed potential, or the opportunity cost of what you didn't do, but could have done, within the existing framework of infrastructure and costs. Businesses obsess over the numbers of what they did, but often ignore the measure of what they could have done!

The key here is to design a customised dashboard for your business that includes numbers you *need* to be looking at on a daily, weekly, monthly and quarterly basis. Not so many that it becomes onerous to produce and contains superfluous information, but not too few so that important stuff gets missed.

We have many examples of relevant dashboards that we have created and worked on with clients in many industries, so feel free to email me at stephen.sacks@fundingnav.com with a brief description of your company and industry type. I will then send you something you can work with that has worked well for a similar business to yours.

As with everything, having the information to hand is all very well, but the real gain is *acting on the numbers*. Without action, you are wasting your time producing them.

Key Points

> » Work out what needs measuring.
> » Make sure it is being measured accurately and in time.
> » Make sure the leadership is being held to account and the elephant in the room is being addressed.
> » Act on what you find.

9

Start With the End in Mind

Venture Capitalists, and to some extent Private Equity, are always totally ruthless, efficient investors, and demand huge performance from the companies in their portfolios. They always start with the end in mind. That is, they don't even consider an investment unless they have a highly profitable exit strategy planned. They then work from point A today to point B, which is their exit, in the quickest and most efficient way, so as to reach it as swiftly as possible and at the least possible cost.

Their decision-making is so much easier than it is for an owner manager, as their end game is always the same: to build and to recirculate their capital every three to five years through creating some kind of transaction. You, on the other hand, as a business owner, may need to consider a series of potential issues before deciding that an ultimate sale is your final goal.

» If you were to sell, would it be for enough to retire on? (Unlikely at current investment returns unless you have an amazing business and a very motivated buyer.)

» Family or staff succession issues.

» Legacy or social issues.

» Whether you have in fact achieved your business goal, which may be aspirational rather than financial.

Based on current returns of around 1.5% pa, you would need to bank £10m after tax to gain an investment income of just £150k pa. Given that a business that sells for north of £10m was probably generating profits of around £1m – £3m pa in the run up to the sale, it doesn't seem such a great deal unless you really need to get out or to access that kind of lump sum for some reason.

You may also consider a partial exit, where management get some skin in the game and work with you to grow the business in the future so that you can continue to draw dividends. This is, of course, fraught with risks that either the business won't run as well or you just won't be able to step back.

Legacy and social issues are very personal. It may be that your great-grandfather started the business a century ago and you feel that it must be passed on to the next generation; or else there is a local or social reason why the business should not be sold.

Whatever the ultimate strategy, it's always a good idea to have it in mind from as early as possible so that the business can be groomed to maximise the value and be encapsulated in a plan.

A strategic plan is a document that establishes the direction of a company or work unit. It can be a single page or fill up a binder, depending on the size and complexity of the business and work.

Most managers would benefit from having their own strategic plan. The process of developing a plan helps the manager (and the team) to step back and examine where they are, where they want to go, and how to get there.

In the absence of a plan, work still gets done on a day-to-day basis but often lacks a sense of purpose and priority.

A Basic, Simplified, Strategic Plan

Here is a template for a basic, simplified, strategic plan that any manager can fill out, providing both long-term purpose and direction, and tactical operating plans. Whilst you could certainly complete the template alone, I recommend a more collaborative approach in order to get buy-in across the company.

Vision Statement

A vision statement is an aspirational statement of where you want your unit to be in the future. 'Future' is usually defined as the next three to five years, but it could be more. A vision should set the overall direction for the unit and team and should be bold and inspirational. A vision describes the '*what*' and the '*why*' for everything you do.

Here is an example vision statement from Zappos, the Amazon subsidiary from Las Vegas:

> '*One day, 30 per cent of all retail transactions in the US will be online. People will buy from the company with the best service and the best selection. Zappos.com will be that online store. Our hope is that our focus on service will allow us to wow our customers, our employees, our vendors, and our investors. We want Zappos.com to be known as a service company that happens to sell shoes, handbags, and anything and everything.*'

Mission Statement

While a vision describes where you want to be in the future, a mission statement describes what you do today. It often describes what you do, for whom, and how. Focusing on your mission each day should enable you to reach your vision. A mission statement could broaden your choices, and/ or narrow them.

Here is an example of a mission statement from Harley-Davidson:

> '*We fulfill dreams through the experience of motorcycling, by providing motorcyclists and the general public with an expanding line of motorcycles and branded products and services in selected market segments.*'

A vision and mission can also be combined in the same statement.

Here is an example from The Walt Disney Company:

'The mission of The Walt Disney Company is to be one of the world's leading producers and providers of entertainment and information. Using our portfolio of brands to differentiate our content, services, and consumer products, we seek to develop the most creative, innovative, and profitable entertainment experiences and related products in the world.'

Note that the statement is both aspirational (*'to be one of the...'*), and descriptive of what they do and how they do it.

Core Values

Core values describe your beliefs and behaviours. They are the things you believe in that will enable you to achieve your vision and mission.

Here is an example of core values from the Coca-Cola Company:

'Leadership: The courage to shape a better future
Collaboration: Leverage collective genius
Integrity: Be real
Accountability: If it is to be, it's up to me
Passion: Committed in heart and mind
Diversity: As inclusive as our brands
Quality: What we do, we do well'.

SWOT Analysis

SWOT stands for *strengths, weaknesses, opportunities* and *threats*. A SWOT analysis sums up where you are now and provides ideas on what you need to focus on.

Long-Term Goals

Long-term goals are three to five statements that drill down a level below the vision and describe how you plan to achieve that vision.

Yearly Objectives

Each long-term goal should have a few (three to five) one-year objectives that advance your goals. Each objective should be as 'SMART' as possible: *Specific, Measurable, Achievable, Realistic,* and *Time-based.*

Action Plans

Each objective should have a plan that details how the objective will be achieved. The amount of detail depends on the complexity of the objective.

Note that the strategic plan starts at the highest level (vision) and then gets more specific. *Both are important.*

It's been said that, *"A vision without a plan is just a dream. A plan without a vision is just drudgery. But a vision with a plan can change the world".*

The fact is that for any of these outcomes to succeed it is key that you, the owner, take progressive steps back in order that management can take on the mantle. So investment in skills and training is key, and trust needs to be built from as early as possible.

Your input should be to work on the business rather than in it from the earliest possible point if you want to maximise its value both to yourself and to any potential acquirer.

Using an external resource such as Funding Nav can be a massive benefit in helping to create both a strategic plan and also a structure that can maximise a business's attractiveness, value and, ultimately, its potential saleability.

It is also helpful to think about stakeholders, and other potential investors' motivation in creating an exit or partial exit. Years ago, I sold a bed linen retail business to an online consolidator who had just acquired a new warehouse/distribution centre and was actively seeking to amortise his investment by adding a volume-based online player to his portfolio, basically in order to fill his warehouse (crazy, I know!). As a result of this, we were able to sell for a considerable premium relative to what we would have got from a purely financial investor.

Key Points

» Make yourself redundant from the day-to-day as quickly as possible and work on improving the business.

» Try to think about your own personal goals and work towards facilitating those from day one.

» If you decide that a sale is your goal, then start to position the business as early as possible in a sweet spot for a potential acquirer. It is helpful if there is more than one potential acquirer as ultimately it takes two to create an auction, which is the only time when prices really accelerate.

» Think seriously about using an external advisor to guide you on your journey and to offer an objective point of view.

» Draw up a strategic plan and use it as a working, live document.

PART 2

RAISING FUNDS

An Introduction to Raising Funds

When I was running SME trading businesses, raising funds was always a challenge. Unlike larger companies that have a whole department called Finance (and maybe one called Treasury too), as well as a myriad of advisors looking to add value, the lonely SME leader needs to add fundraising to his or her long, required list of skills.

Apart from a lack of advice and possibly options, SME leaders also have less value at their disposal. It always makes me laugh when I hear government banging on about how the small business sector is the engine of the economy, yet they prevail over a situation where larger businesses can borrow at a few points over base, and where the CEO gets an enormous salary for taking absolutely no personal risk at all.

In the so-called 'engine' in this gleaming example of double-standard economic management, however, the leader is saddled with two issues:

1. Debt costs substantially more than it does for larger businesses; often more than twice as much.

2. It is generally expected and accepted that, in the event of the enterprise failing, the director(s) will repay the debt, even at the cost of their own family home, through the signing of rather onerous personal guarantees that totally remove the protection of limited liability from them.

So, the so-called 'highly-valued' entrepreneurs of our small-business-powered economy are doubly disadvantaged, and sometimes permanently financially crippled by this ridiculous situation, whilst the leaders of larger businesses are richly rewarded regardless of their risk exposure. Most ridiculously of all, the leaders of our banks are able to get the government to underwrite their errors and have the tax payer bail their banks out, whilst they continue to draw multi-million-pound salaries regardless of their errors.

Now, admittedly Antonio Horta Osorio, the CEO of *Lloyds Bank*, wasn't responsible for the problems the bank found itself in after its disastrous takeover of HBOS in the teeth of the financial crisis, as he only took over in 2011. Nonetheless, he soon managed to find himself in the midst of a nervous breakdown as he got to grips with the issues that it caused. But he still had his multi-million-pound salary, even after a small cut following his extra-marital affair with Wendy Piatt and a trip to *The Priory* to sort his head out. Now, just imagine if he'd also had to cope with the prospect of no salary, the bank foreclosing on his house, and no money to afford the luxury of private rehab normally reserved for celebrities, as the cost of potential failure. The mental anxiety that paralysed him as he fought to deal with the bank's issues would have been multiplied and his ability to gain support reduced. The outcome could have been tragic!

Well, guess what, Antonio's bank has a whole department that is designed specifically to force failed entrepreneurs out of their houses, and potentially bankrupt them if their companies are unable to repay loans that were taken out with guarantees secured over the family home. Yet it sees no irony in taking bailouts from the government for its own lack of judgement, sending its CEO to *The Priory* for stress issues, whilst at the same time foreclosing on its SME customers and, in some cases, taking their family homes for itself while claiming to be supportive to business. Go figure!

OK, rant over!! But that, in a nutshell, was my motivation for launching Funding Nav.

I wanted to create a resource that SME company owners could turn to that would advise them on:

1. Their case for funding and indeed where there are other free alternatives, such as with the snack company example earlier.
2. Whether borrowing is the correct route, and then where to go at least cost and risk.
3. How to deal with aggressive lenders if their back is against the wall.

It's actually quite complex, and I've found in my own experience in business that local advisors and accountants are often ill-advised themselves. Generally, there isn't just a single answer to a funding question but a myriad of alternatives that are sometimes complimentary and sometimes conflicting. They are ever-changing and therefore it is key that directors are abreast of new innovations and ideas.

Now, having slagged off the UK's small business infrastructure from a debt perspective, I will say that, from a tax and regulations perspective, it is one of the *best places in the world* to equity fund a business, run a business and sell a business. Sometimes when we are advising overseas interests on strategy, one of the first suggestions we make is that they incorporate and fund a UK-based business, and then use that as a holding company to acquire their overseas interests.

The mixture of SEIS, EIS, very advanced crowdfunding and angel networks, low rates of corporate tax, R&D tax credits and entrepreneur's relief on the sale of an enterprise make the UK unbelievably attractive from this perspective.

I have attempted to set out here an explanation of and a reference to many of the terms used in the industry, and to explain some of the ideas that we regularly use at Funding Nav in order to deliver enterprises our promise of getting them funding. This is, however, by no means comprehensive, as space dictates, but it is certainly a good start. Again, I'm happy to respond to readers' specific enquiries about their own company situation by email at stephen.sacks@fundingnav.com.

Now, there are essentially *five ways* to increase the working capital available to you within your business:

1. Retaining more profits

2. Better managing the cash flow

3. Free cash sources

4. Equity

5. Debt

Obviously options 1 to 3 are a given as prudent management techniques, and 1 and 2 are covered off specifically in section 3 of this book. What I will do, therefore, in this section, is focus specifically on external cash resources* that you should investigate fully before committing yourself to a particular strategy.

---

*The following information listed under the Grants section has been sourced from https:// entrepreneurhandbook.co.uk/grants-loans/ and was accurate at the time of print.

10

Free Cash

R&D Tax Credits

The UK rate of corporation tax (on profits) is already at a historical low of 19% at the time of writing, but for companies that invest in risky or novel ideas that relate to their products, services or processes, further discounts or even refunds are allowed. These are particularly generous for small to medium-sized businesses with under 500 employees. Effectively, they allow the claiming company to multiply their relevant costs by 2.3 for accounting purposes only, and to go back and reclaim the last two financial years.

This is by no means an easy process and certainly not automated like payroll taxes and sales taxes, which are calculated simply and arithmetically. Successful reclaim of R&D requires the company to submit both a narrative case to HMRC setting out the story behind the project, and the allowable costs. It is highly subjective and is best undertaken by an external consultant who does this all the time. R&D reclaim demands a lot of lateral thinking, and some of the more successful claims that Funding Nav have completed for clients on a 'no win no fee' basis have related to failed projects that were subsequently canned. This is because failure is great proof that the project was risky, but there is R&D to be found across businesses in surprising places.

We have managed to reclaim six-figure sums for businesses as diverse as cafés, TV production, recruitment and fashion companies. It is interesting that there is normally internal resistance from the FD when we suggest it because they don't really understand how to maximise the impact of R&D reclaims. I suppose sometimes they are also reticent because they feel they should have suggested it themselves.

Some industries, such as video games and film, have enhanced schemes, and businesses that hold patents are able to register for the patent box scheme, which is a very generous tax break ongoing.

The government are pretty keen on paying out under this scheme as they see, on average, £6 in additional taxation raised over time by companies that have reclaimed R&D for every £1 that they paid out, because obviously research, development and innovation generally drive higher profitability and more employment and tax-take over time.

Again, please *email me personally* at stephen.sacks@fundingnav.com if you want to discuss your specific case.

Grants

Whilst R&D is a pretty common if somewhat underused resource, grants are an *increasingly rare commodity*. This has nothing to do with their availability, as you can see from the somewhat lengthy list featured here, but more to do with the perceived difficulty of obtaining this enormously valuable resource of free cash.

As with R&D tax credits, the devil is definitely in the detail in applying for what is generally government money to subsidise your venture. Writing the application is a key and lengthy task that should really be done by someone who is experienced, with a comprehensive understanding of the vagaries of the system.

Please *email me* at stephen.sacks@fundingnav.com if you have a project that you believe deserves grant funding. I can then let you know next steps and indeed if this is a worthwhile or likely opportunity for your business.

Meanwhile, here is a pretty comprehensive list of what's currently available, but bear in mind that the position with grant money is that it's highly fluid, and schemes open and close frequently and often without notice. All the funding details below were correct at the time this book went to print. However, if you notice that any grants are no longer available, then please either search in your browser or head over to www. fundingnav.com for the latest information.

Innovate UK: Innovation Grants Programmes

Innovate UK is the official innovation agency for the UK government. As such, it runs a range of national and European funding programmes providing grants to support UK businesses who are on the cutting edge of innovation and technology. The principal funding programmes and innovation grant initiatives are detailed below. Under these programmes, each year calls for businesses from different sectors/stages/technologies are put out, and active grants are usually listed.

Innovation Vouchers

Innovation Vouchers provide a relatively small but useful government grant to develop an innovative idea or new product by giving you expert know-how. Innovate UK will help you source the right expert for your business from one of the following:

Universities and FE colleges

Technology and Research institutions

Consultancies and Catapult centres

Advisors on design

IP Advisors

Funding: £5,000 to pay for externally-based experts and consultants to grow your business.

Launchpads

The Launchpads grant funding competitions are for companies looking to turn new, innovative and exciting ideas into viable commercial projects. The grants are primarily for businesses in specific areas of the country and are allocated three times a year (these change intermittently, so check the site).

To be eligible for a Launchpads grant you need to be a small or medium-sized business in the early stages of development, working in the technology industry, be in an applicable geographical cluster or be planning to move there, and have ambitions to grow your company.

Funding: up to £100,000, but you must be able to match the grant amount with the same amount of private or self-funding.

Small Business Research Initiative (SBRI)

The SBRI provides contracts and funding for businesses to carry out research into, or the development of, new products or services for the public sector. The programme aims to fund innovative ideas that can enhance public services or solve a specific public-sector problem. Any business is eligible to apply for an SBRI contract or grant.

Funding: initial funding is between £50,000 and £100,000, with additional funding of up to £1,000,000 to develop your project or idea further.

Smart Grants

The Smart Grants scheme provides grants for start-ups researching and creating significant technological or scientific breakthroughs.

Three kinds of Smart Grant are available:

1. Proof of Market, 60% match funds, £25,000.

2. Proof of Concept, 60% match funds, £100,000.

3. Prototype Development, 45% match funds, £250,000.

The level you apply for depends on the stage of your company, your finances and what you are looking to develop. You will need to be an early stage business, have serious growth ambitions and work in the technology, science or engineering fields.

Funding: £25,000 – £250,000.

Knowledge Transfer Partnerships (KTP)

KTP grants are awarded to businesses who employ recent graduates working on innovation projects. Graduates must be working in coordination with, and supervised by, a research partner. The grant is open to businesses large and small, but the percentage of funding varies depending on size of project and the project itself. Other than that, to be eligible for a KTP award, you must be a UK business, charity, educational institution or private/public sector research organisation.

Funding: up to 67% of project costs. Larger businesses may only apply for up to 50%. A limit on the financing is not stipulated but is assumed.

Feasibility Studies

Feasibility Studies grants will support you in testing a new business idea to see if it will work. This includes new product development, a new process or business model development, and service development. To qualify, you must be a United Kingdom-based research organisation or business and be able to showcase your final project at a national collaboration event. Your proposals must be business focused and meet the theme of the grant.

Funding: 70% grant funded up to the amount of £400,000 (research organisations can get up to 100% depending on the project).

Eurostars

The Eurostars programme is a European Union funding project led locally by Innovate UK. Eurostars grants provide funding for the development and research of innovative services, products or processes. You can work with partners in other European projects to collaborate on funding proposals.

To be eligible for a Eurostars grant, you must be a small to medium-sized business in the UK, be working in the tech industry and have the intention of collaborating with other European companies. (Large companies can still participate in Eurostars projects but must self-fund.)

Funding: 50% match-funded grants with up to £300,000 in funding available.

Horizon 2020

Horizon 2020 is a massive EU fund designed to support SMEs all across Europe. You can access funding calls through some UK government agencies and organisations.

The funding can be used to:

» Create something too enormous to build alone.

» Work with companies throughout a value chain.

» Create access to technology and science.

» Find and draw on skills and expertise that you need.

» Investigate opportunities to test innovative ideas and solutions.

Funding: bids can range from £100,000 to £10,000,000 plus. Horizon 2020 has a complicated bidding process, with several different grant calls going out at any one time, as well as various delivery agencies. The grant is focused on EU inclusion, so it is likely you will have to bid with at least one other company from another member country of the European Union.

Collaborative Research and Development

The Collaborative grants scheme endeavours to push forward the boundaries of technology by providing significant grant funding to fund/accelerate research and development programmes of UK organisations developing new products, services or processes.

To qualify for collaborative R&D grants, you must be a UK research organisation or business, be working in science, technology or engineering industries, and be collaborating with a fellow research partner or company.

Funding: grants can be up to 60% of total cost and between £25,000 and £5,000,000 in amount.

Catalysts

The Catalyst grant programme is designed to fund initiatives invested in creating new knowledge or developing groundbreaking/innovative products, services or processes. Innovate UK runs four different Catalyst programmes including Industrial Biotechnology, Energy, Argi-Tech and Biomedical.

To be eligible for a grant, you must be a UK business, thinking of starting a UK business, working in one of the four Catalyst areas and working with a fellow business or research partner on the project. There are three core stages of funding including early stage (feasibility studies), industrial research (prototype) and late stage (testing).

Funding: 60% of total costs with an overall grant award of between £150,000 and £10,000,000. The funding levels vary depending on the stage of your business and project.

Apprenticeship Grant

Apprenticeship Grants support work and training designed to meet the needs of employers. They take between one and four years to complete and bring together practical training with job-based learning.

Funding: the National Apprentice Service may give funds for training. The quantity of funding depends on your business area, with funding for 16- to 18-year-olds beginning at 100%. You may also have access to an Apprentice Grant of up to £1,500 (ten employees max), which is for employers taking on apprentices aged 16 to 24.

The Prince's Countryside Fund

Set up to help rural communities in the UK face modern challenges, the Prince's Countryside Fund provides grant funding to projects that have a long-term positive impact in regard to assisting entrepreneurs to work and live in the British countryside.

The grants are provided to businesses or organisations who seek to increase the potential return and longevity of family-run farm businesses, sustain and grow rural economies, or provide necessary aid to support areas hit by hardship (for more details on this check out the Grant Eligibility and Guidance document).

Funding: up to £50,000 per project (with more than £1,000,000 in funding being awarded each year).

Grants for the Arts

The Arts Council have been funding creative projects across England for decades, providing grants to organisations running a vast range of art and cultural initiatives.

Grants for the Arts is a funding programme to support art organisations and individuals in visual arts, dance, theatre, literature, music and more. To be eligible, you must be furthering art and culture, creating a long-term impact and providing a project that is accessible to anyone, e.g. a play at the theatre or an art installation. To date, the Arts Council has given out £1.5 billion in funding and grants to projects.

Funding: £1,000 – £100,000. (Your project can be funded up to 90% by this grant.)

Grant for Business Investment (GBI – RDA)

The GBI is a capital grant offered by the Regional Development Agencies (RDAs). The grants are mainly intended to help businesses expand and diversify their perspectives. They can assist entrepreneurs to set up a new company or fund a new project. The grants are given to high-budget projects whose outcomes can be evaluated on a long-term basis. They are often dedicated to funding projects that can bring prosperity to economically deprived areas, and are especially granted to offshore wind manufacturing projects. You can apply for the grant directly from the GBI website.

Funding: the minimum financing offered is £10,000. The grants are available for businesses of all sizes with a different ratio of funding.

The FedEx Small Business Grant

Initially arriving in the UK in 2016, the FedEx Small Business Grant is a general funding award being offered to UK small and medium businesses, with less than 100 employees, that have been in operation for two or more years. (The 2018 scheme has now closed but I would expect 2019 to open shortly at https://smallbusinessgrant.fedex.com/#/.)

The initial stage of the application requires you to submit details about your business dreams and goals to FedEx online. Business plans will be requested from a shortlist of companies, and winners of the grant will be announced.

Funding: a main grant of £20,000, with smaller grants of £5,000 for two runners-up.

Tradeshow Access Programme (TAP)

TAP has been set up to help UK businesses promote themselves abroad. It provides grants for companies to visit trade shows overseas, assisting businesses to attain foreign exposure, gain market knowledge, and access the advice/support of international trade experts.

To be eligible for TAP, you must be attending an event listed on the official TAP calendar and be a UK SME. You must also already be exploring export opportunities and be a new exporter (export accounts for less than 25% of your business). Additionally, your business must have been exporting for less than ten years, be under the state aid limit, not be receiving any other public funds towards the trade show, and not have confirmed attendance at the tradeshow before applying for the grant.

Apart from the core eligibility criteria, you will also have to show you are either selling services/products from the UK, or that you are adding a significant amount of value to a product/service not coming from the UK.

Funding: £500 to £2,500 is available. You must 100% match the grant received from Trade Challenge Partner towards the cost of attending/ exhibiting at the tradeshow.

Arts Council England Funding

The Arts Council runs a rolling grants programme to support cultural, art and theatre events and other creative initiatives. The grants are reasonably substantial and are open for application by both organisations and individuals (there is no limitation on for-profit companies).

The Arts Council grant scheme is perfect for organisations that are undertaking creative projects as part of their primary activity, for instance theatre companies, art galleries and more. Larger corporations could take advantage of the programme to completely or partially fund cultural or art initiatives that have a meaningful impact, or aim to further and preserve long-term British culture or art.

To apply, you will need to create an account with the Arts Council website and build your profile. You will then have to wait for your account to be verified before taking an eligibility questionnaire and starting your application. It is not a quick grant programme, with answers beyond application taking from six to 12 weeks, but it is one of the clearest and easiest-to-follow funding processes available for UK organisations.

Funding: £1,000 to £100,000 (grant requests of £15,000 or below take six weeks or less to get a decision; grants over £15,000 take 12 weeks or more to get a decision).

Barrow Cadbury Trust Grants

One of the oldest charitable trusts in the UK, the Barrow Cadbury Trust's aim is to bring about social change. It funds projects that will generate significant and sustainable change for the better in society, creating more equality across migration, criminal justice and economic justice.

The Economic Justice grant programme is the most relevant programme for businesses seeking a grant if the project you propose is focused on reducing economic inequality between the richest and the poorest in society. With historical links in Birmingham, organisations in that area will also have an added advantage in applying.

Before proceeding, you will need to consider if your project/proposal fits within the criteria of the Economic Justice programme. Then fill in an application form with your goals, measures and theory of how you can create change through the project. Once you have supplied these details, expect a reply within ten days as to whether you have progressed and should begin making a full application.

Funding: amounts of funding are not specified but, given the history, expect small to significant grants to be made available, based on varying projects and outcomes.

British Council Grants

The British Council issue grants on a rolling basis through a range of funding programmes, including the Newton Fund and Artists International Development Fund.

Funding amounts vary widely programme to programme.

Newton Fund

The Newton Fund fosters innovation and research partnerships between players in different countries by providing grant funding for research, workshops and travel. In this pursuit, the fund issues funding calls/programmes on a rolling basis. These programmes have different criteria and focus on various countries/endeavours. You will find a list of the latest Newton Fund programmes on their website on the funding and other opportunities page.

As an example of the type of programmes they support, please find below a list of current grant calls:

» Gulf Science Innovation and Knowledge Economy

» Creative Economy – Project Evaluation and Guide

» Building strong data management, data repository and curation systems

» Promote your research/institution in Germany

Funding: varies grant to grant.

Develop & Fund Your Creativity

This fund is focused on fostering innovation and development within the creative industries, including art, fashion, design and more, with a further focus on the development of young people in these sectors, coupled with collaboration between countries and cultures. Within this area, grants and programmes run on a rolling basis, with new calls coming out regularly. The majority are business relevant, including the Artists' International Development Fund and Shorts Support Scheme.

Funding: varies grant to grant.

Big Lottery Fund

The Big Lottery Fund provides a range of grants that are mostly focused towards delivering community or charity funding, with the aim of instigating social change. However, some programmes, including those listed below, are available to for-profits, community interest companies and social businesses. The grants tend to range from £300 to £500,000 or more.

Grants for Improving Lives

The Improving Lives programme aims to fund socially-focused organisations working with people who have overcome some form of difficulty in their lives and built up resilience. The programme area is limited to Scotland and it's most relevant to businesses in the education, therapeutic or other industries.

Funding: £10,000 to £1,000,000 in total funding. Grants over £150,000 require a two-stage process and a further application form. (Grants above £500,000 are not routinely considered but are more likely to be accepted if they have some match funding in place.)

People and Places: large and medium grants

This grant programme is dedicated to providing funding for projects where people and organisations are working together in their local community to bring about change and a positive impact. ***It covers Wales only.***

The programme is limited in applicant scope, only allowing certain types of business to apply, including community interest companies (CIC), social enterprises and not-for-profits.

Funding: £10,001 to £500,000 (medium grants funded up to £100,000, large grants up to £500,000).

Youth Investment Fund

The Youth Investment Fund provides funding to community organisations, social enterprises and youth groups to deliver high quality youth services in areas across England. Successful applicants are funded for several years, allowing investment in the future and in sustainability. Organisations applying for grants in disadvantaged areas are most likely to receive funding.

Funding: £150,000 to £700,000.

Power to Change Community Business Fund

The Power to Change Fund is designed purely to support community-based businesses in the UK. This means businesses run by local people for local people and, in the process, protecting local services and meeting local needs.

Aside from social entities, community interest companies and charities, they do fund limited companies but are very strict on the community criteria. Take a closer look at the four essential features of a community business.

To apply, apart from the above, you will need to propose a project beyond your usual line of business, provide a year's full accounting information, and be able to fund part of your project from another source.

Funding: £50,000 to £300,000. (They will not fund projects to 100%. You will require some other source of internal or external finance to put towards the project proposed.)

Forestry Commission

The Forest Commission run a range of funding and grant schemes designed to expand, protect and promote the sustainable management of woodlands in British society. These grants are highly focused on businesses and organisations involved in land management and woodland. Details of open funding schemes can be found below. (Closed and legacy grant schemes include: FWS and FWPS payment rates, Woodland Grant Scheme, Farm Woodland Scheme, Farm Woodland Premium Scheme and the English Woodland Grant scheme.)

Forestry Innovation Fund (DEFRA)

The Forestry Innovation Fund is a national fund put together by DEFRA with more than £1,000,000 available to fund projects that promote the growth of the forestry industry within an applicant organisation's local region.

Funding: not detailed.

Country Stewardship

As part of the RDPE programme, the Countryside Stewardship Scheme comprises nearly £900,000,000 in grants and funding opportunities that will be made available to UK woodland managers and farmers for the foreseeable future.

This fund is to support farmers and woodland managers to look after the environment, including in tasks such as creating new woodland, solving tree health issues, acting in support of management plans for the government and improving existing woodlands. A decision tree can be found on their website detailing the different types of Stewardship funding you could access depending on your proposal.

Funding: not detailed, assumed substantial.

Woodland Creation Planning Grant (WCPG)

WCPG provides contributions in the form of grants to land managers collecting and analysing information for productive multi-purpose woodland proposals, including any impacts on water, biodiversity, historic environment and more.

To be eligible, the applicant business or individual will need at least ten hectares of land, for 70% or more of species in the proposed area to be productive, and for at least one woodland block on the land to be more than ten hectares, with any further blocks being a minimum of five hectares. The land applied for must also be in the England.

Funding: £1,000 for initial land assessment and data collection, with a further £150 per hectare (the initial £1,000 is incorporated into the overall payment).

Unltd Social Enterprise Funding

Initially based in the UK, Unltd has become a global and influential partner and investor for social entrepreneurs, social businesses and social enterprise across the world. They run a range of grant, support and award programmes to help entrepreneurs all the way through, from setting up a new venture to scaling. Below is a list of currently active grant programmes we have identified as good for socially-minded businesses.

Transform Ageing

The Transform Ageing programme aims to drastically improve the approach and services we provide to society when dealing with the elderly, from a social care, health and wellbeing point of view.

The programme provides support for businesses and organisations who work in several core areas of focus/innovation, including developing or providing solutions for the elderly that create positive experiences, enhance independence through transportation or mobility, support carers, make relevant information more accessible, and support people in making life changes or creating opportunities for connection.

The programme itself is separate from any funding, but you can apply under the programme criteria for one of the Unltd award schemes. An eligibility criterion is detailed on the site. Aside from pure financing, you can get expert advice and support right through to making your idea a reality or scaling your social organisation.

Funding: £0 to £25,000. (The early stage awards do not list an amount of funding. If any, it is assumed small. However, the venture level awards provide up to £25,000 in funding to established organisations.)

Spaces 4 Change

The Spaces 4 Change programme aims to support young social entrepreneurs in taking ownership of vacant or under-utilised spaces in their local area for use as offices or retail outlets for new social ventures.

To be eligible for the programme, you need to be aged between 16 and 24, must be based in the UK, must apply as an informal group or individual, and have a clear project plan in place with specific outcomes.

Funding: up to £5,000.

Do It Awards

In their own words, the Do It Awards are here to 'help you to create more positive social impact'. They are designed to provide one-to-one support, expert advice and a range of resources for young social entrepreneurs who want to turn their ideas into thriving social ventures.

Funding: monetary finance isn't detailed. However, they do say it's included, although it's unclear what form this investment would take. Best to ask before applying!

Grow It Awards

The Grow It Awards are for social entrepreneurs who are focused on growing their venture and are seeking tailored support, expertise and further funding (this award replaces the Unltd previous programme of Fast Growth and Build It Awards).

To be eligible, you will need to meet the Unltd criteria both as an entrepreneur and as a venture. As well as a monetary award, if successful you will get expert advice, plus access to investors, corporations and other entrepreneurs, coupled with 12 months of free coaching.

Funding: £15,000.

Better Broadband Subsidy Scheme

With a focus on the current and future growth of the digital economy, the British government is trying to increase the number of businesses that can access high-speed broadband and internet. The Better Broadband Subsidy Scheme is part of that initiative and, as such, offers subsidies to businesses for installation of broadband if they cannot get access to affordable internet providing a minimum speed of 2mb.

This grant is most useful for businesses in remote areas that do not have access to standard broadband or fibre optic, allowing you to avoid paying for expensive and comparatively slow satellite internet.

Funding: up to £350.

Sustainable Routes

A government-funded initiative, Sustainable Routes creates travel efficiency plans for individuals and businesses to cut down on travel time, mileage costs and CO2 output. They also offer grants towards the cost of creating and implementing a travel efficiency plan in the workplace. All businesses are eligible, particularly those interested in reducing their environmental impact while cutting travel costs.

Funding: up to £1,000.

Energy Entrepreneurs Fund

The Energy Entrepreneurs Fund is a grant funding programme to support the advancement and presentation of cutting-edge technologies, processes and products in the core sectors of power production, electricity, heat storage and energy efficiency.

The scheme overall seeks the advancement of energy technology by assisting SMEs monetarily as well as with other benefits, including incubation space and expert support. Phase 6 of the fund has recently been launched and is over £10,000,000.

To be successful, applicants will need to present hard evidence to support their case for funding. This will include, but not be limited to, the likely impact of their project on 2050 low carbon targets, the scope and precise nature of the business opportunity, the value for money and further cost reduction, and the overall technical viability of the project, as well as a detailed roadmap for development.

Funding: up to £1,000,000.

Trusthouse Charitable Foundation

The Foundation provides a range of grant funding programmes to support large UK organisations that can solve local issues in areas of significant urban deprivation, or isolated and vicarious rural communities. Within these two core areas, the foundation is most interested in projects within disability and healthcare, community support and art, heritage and education.

To be eligible, your organisation and project must be based in the UK. You must also be a CIC, social enterprise, a not-for-profit registered company or charity to be a grant recipient. It is typical for small grants to receive a final decision within six weeks of applying.

Funding: grants are split into three sizes/tiers including up to £6,000, £6,001 to £12,000 and £12,001 to £45,000. (Typically they require that you put up at least 50% of the total project costs to be considered for a grant.)

Biffaward

This is designed to support not-for-profit companies who are looking to improve their local community by starting or growing projects in the fields of recreation, cultural facilities, rebuilding, biodiversity and community buildings.

Biffaward eligibility varies based on the area your project is in. Check the website for more specific details.

Funding: up to £199,000 in total project costs. (Typical grant sizes are not exampled but assume some level of match funding is required above small grants levels.)

The Carbon Trust Green Business Fund

The Carbon Trust operates the Green Business Fund, which covers a certain amount of capital costs for medium and small businesses in the UK when buying energy-reducing or saving equipment.

The grant scheme covers the entirety of the UK (minus Northern Ireland). To be eligible, you will need to purchase equipment from a Green Business Directory or BESA supplier. The funding is on a first come, first served basis until it runs out.

Funding: up to 15% of total project costs, with a maximum grant of £5,000.

Architectural Heritage Fund (AHF)

The AHF established in 1986 is dedicated to promoting and supporting the conservation and re-use of historic buildings to the advantage of local communities across the UK. With this overall objective in mind, AHF is one of the UK's leading social investors, offering a range of grants, loans, advice and much more.

For a project to be eligible for a grant, it must have the potential to create significant economic and social benefits for a deprived or in need community. You must be able to demonstrate the social and heritage impact of your project, and also be registered as a charity or social enterprise with a limited liability structure. In addition, you need to prove that you have a clear and attainable roadmap to project completion. It's advisable to speak to an AHF grants officer before making an application online.

Funding: £0 to £5,000 and £5,000+. (Smaller grant applications receive a decision in six weeks, with larger applications being decided on a quarterly basis by the board. Applications that are already match funded to 50% or above are given priority.)

Discover England Fund

A £40m fund run by Discover England designed to support their tourism industry in being competitive on an international landscape, the fund mainly promotes inbound tourism. There is an emphasis on encouraging tourists to explore other parts of the UK, not just London, through creating better transport links and offering customers easy booking options online.

Grants are delivered for small-scale pilot and large-scale collaborative projects. To be eligible for a grant award, you will need to be creating or providing a world-class tourism product or service.

Funding: not stipulated, but likely dependent on project size. (It is a massive government grant project so also assume some requirement for match funding.)

Low-emission vehicles eligible for a Plug-in Grant

The Plug-in Grant allows auto manufacturers and dealers to apply to get grant funding to reduce the price a business/individual will pay for any given car that meets government emission/electric conditions. Thus, the overall price to the customer is reduced and more sales for dealerships and manufacturers are generated.

To be eligible, you will need to be a car dealership or manufacturer, and you will have to apply on behalf of the customer. Vehicles available for a grant include select category 1, 2 and 3 cars, as well as motorcycles, mopeds, hybrids and vans (a Plug-in Van Grant may be better).

Funding: 35% of the purchase price up to a maximum of £4,500 on eligible vehicles.

Fuel Cell Electric Vehicle Fleet Support Scheme

The scheme is an initiative run by the UK government to accelerate the growth of the commercial market of Hydrogen fuel cell electric vehicles. The Fuel Cell Electric Vehicle Fleet Support Scheme provides grants to public sector and private sector organisations, including private company grants to buy FCEVs. (The main difference between private and public sector grants is that there is no cap to the grant for public sector organisations acquiring these vehicles.)

Funding: for private companies, you can get a maximum of £200,000 per business to cover up to 75% of the cost of acquiring a fleet of FCEVs, including fleet management, car insurance, fuel, project reporting and more. It is a £2,000,000 fund and will close when exhausted.

Fit For Nuclear

Developed by Nuclear AMRC, Fit For Nuclear is a programme that works with manufacturing firms to get them ready for bidding to carry out work in the civilian nuclear supply chain in the UK. The overall plan culminates in making a funding application for a grant.

The scheme is aimed at companies with no atomic experience that are involved in high-level precision mechanical engineering, supply of instrumentation and control, electrical components or production of other manufactured devices for nuclear plant operation, construction or decommission.

Businesses eligible for the programme are those that have ten employees or more, or greater than £16,000,000 in turnover annually (the process will be complicated for micro-enterprises, but those with exciting products or services should get in touch). The overall programme will take 12 to 18 months to complete.

Funding: not stipulated.

World of Opportunity SME Grants Programme

To celebrate more than 20 years of the Heathrow Business Summit, Heathrow Airport has established a grants scheme to offer small grants to support growing businesses in travelling to new export markets.

The World of Opportunity SME Grants Programme provides up to 20 SMEs with funding awards to support trade missions, international trade show attendance or market research abroad.

Funding: up to £2,000.

CRACK IT Challenges

The CRACK IT Challenges are a series of grants in the form of challenges supporting a partnership between academic organisations and SMEs to solve business and scientific challenges while delivering commercial benefit (in effect, the rapid researching and commercialisation of new technologies).

The principal funder of the grants scheme is the NC3Rs and the challenges are developed by NC3Rs and programme sponsors. Check the site for the latest challenges. You can apply for a single-phase challenge, a double-stage challenge or even submit a challenge idea.

Funding: depending on the challenge, contract up to £1,000,000 over three years.

Industrial Partnership Awards (IPA)

The IPAs promote collaboration between industry and academically inclined research organisations, with all projects being academically led. There is a detailed eligibility page you should read.

Funding: you or a partner must contribute at least 10% of the overall project cost; the grant can cover the rest.

Innovative Medicines Initiative (IMI)

The IMI's primary objective is to increase the development speed of innovative medicines and patient access to these medicines, particularly in areas where social or medical needs are currently unmet.

The programme develops medicines, vaccines and treatments such as next-generation antibiotics. The grants aspects of the programme support third party organisations, including SMEs, universities and patent organisations, in participating in its projects. The grant can take the form of providing personnel, covering other direct costs, a one-off financial contribution and free subcontracting.

Given the highly detailed nature of the programme, you will need to check out the more advanced IMI2 rules before making an application.

Funding: dependent on the project and organisation.

Access to Work Funding

The Access to Work Funding scheme provides financial support to disabled people who have a paid job, are about to return to a paid position or start a business. With starting a business in mind, if reasonable adjustments

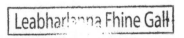

have been made by you as an employer and you have further needs, then the fund can support you in financing special equipment for work, or transport for getting to and from a work location.

To be eligible you must have a health condition or disability that makes it difficult for you to carry out or travel to or from your job, you must be over 16 years of age and live in the UK (Northern Ireland has a different scheme).

Funding: no limit specified (assumed maximum below £10,000).

Britten-Pears Foundation

The Britten-Pears Foundation supplies grant funding to a range of initiatives involved in music, pacifist and local causes. Concerning grants for music, the foundation has funded many musical projects over the years, including composition retreats and much more. They're currently reviewing funding calls, so make sure to check the website for the latest programmes. The grant programmes are most likely to be relevant for music-based businesses.

Funding: not stipulated.

Business Rates Relief

Many businesses pay business rates to their local council, and many are eligible for discounts in the form of business rates relief. Discounting schemes vary from council to council.

There are several core types of business rates relief that can reduce or even exempt your business from paying business rates, including small business rates relief, hardship relief, enterprise zone relief, charitable relief and rural rate relief.

Funding: 0 to 100% reduction in business rates payable.

List of Local Government Grants for Small Businesses

Local authorities and local enterprise authorities work across the United Kingdom to provide a range of funding and grant opportunities to businesses in different geographic areas. In the list below, you will find details of local government grants available for small and medium-sized businesses. This includes the details of each programme, criteria, funding amount and area of coverage. You can look through the list or use the search function in your browser to find the entries covering your city, town, county or country within the United Kingdom.

England

Start-Up Ready

The Tower Hamlets Council offers a grant for new start-up businesses. To be able to apply, you will need to submit an application form to Start-Up Ready, and you must attend and complete the council's four-day start-up programme course.

Funding: £5,000.

Coverage: London Borough of Tower Hamlets, Greater London.

AVDC Business Grant

Aylesbury Vale-based established businesses (i.e. those trading for more than a year) can apply for grant projects that help businesses continue to improve their performance and grow. Once the application is received, it is evaluated to see whether the company is eligible or not. For enquiries or if you qualify and would like to receive an application form, you can email economicdevelopment@aylesburyvaledc.gov.uk.

Funding: the AVDC Business Grant can award a maximum of £5,000 for existing businesses (trading for more than a year), covering up to 50% of the cost (excluding VAT). Turnover is expected to exceed 10% per year from the date the grant is awarded.

Coverage: Aylesbury Vale, Buckinghamshire.

Business Start-Up Grant

Start-up businesses in Aylesbury Vale (i.e. those trading for at least three months or up to a year) can apply for grants aimed at improving their business performance and growth. The maximum number of employees you should have is 30. The fund director is Aylesbury Vale District Council.

Funding: the AVDC business fund can award a maximum of £3,000 to help early-stage businesses to improve business performance and growth, paying up to two-thirds of the cost.

Coverage: Aylesbury Vale, Buckinghamshire.

Elmbridge Civic Improvement Fund (ECIF)

The ECIF has been put in place to help grow the Elmbridge economy by providing funds to improve empty shop fronts and renovate retail businesses.

To apply for the grant, you must be able to show that your project will benefit the local economy or attract people to local amenities and services. Work or purchases the grant could cover include street furniture, improving the appearance of empty shops, street improvements and more.

Funding: £500 to £15,000. You can get up to 90% of the overall project cost.

Coverage: Elmbridge Borough, Surrey.

Elmbridge Start-Up Fund

The Start-Up Fund provides a single grant to help businesses with starting out. This could include buying equipment, marketing, promotion and any initial start-up expenses. To be eligible, businesses must be set up in the Elmbridge area and be no more than six months old.

Funding: £1,000.

Coverage: Elmbridge Borough, Surrey.

Business Support Grant

The Business Support Grant initiative is designed to support local businesses wishing to grow or start new ventures.

Businesses with less than four employees in the Reigate and Banstead Borough area are eligible to apply and you will need to provide a business plan for review. If successful, you will be invited to an interview at the town hall.

Funding: up to £1,000.

Coverage: Reigate and Banstead Borough, Surrey.

Incentive to Grow Grant

Run by Eastleigh Borough Council, the Incentive to Grow Grant is a small monetary grant for new and existing small businesses. The grant can be used for hiring new staff, buying equipment, and marketing. To be eligible for the grant, you must live in the borough of Eastleigh and be, or become, a member of the Southern Entrepreneurs Association.

Funding: £500, up to 50% match funded to the total cost of the project.

Coverage: Eastleigh Borough, Hampshire.

Business Incentive Grant

The Business Incentive Grant is designed to support start-up businesses in the Test Valley in building a competitive local economy. To be eligible for the grant, you must apply before you start your business and you must be working on the business full time. You must also be prepared to receive two site visits from the council to the premises you're operating your business from, as well as providing the necessary paperwork. The whole process, unfortunately, is rather long and will take six months or more.

Funding: up to £750.

Coverage: Test Valley, Hampshire.

Independent Retailer Grant

Test Valley Council is intent on encouraging independent retail companies to take up unused and vacant spaces in the towns of Andover and Romsey. This encouragement takes the form of grants to cover rent for existing and new businesses moving into ground-level vacant properties in the town centres.

Funding: £1,000 (payment is in stages with £500 paid in the first three months and a further £500 paid nine months later).

Coverage: Andover and Romsey, Hampshire.

Small Business Grant

Run by the local business partnership, the Small Business Grant is designed to provide general funding for small and micro businesses in the Adur and Worthing area for specific projects or acquisitions that will make a difference to their business.

To be eligible for the Small Business Grant, your business must have no more than ten employees, be located in the Adur and Worthing area, and be able to justify how the grant funding will develop or further establish your business.

Funding: you can apply for matched grant funding of up to £2,500, meaning you must also be able to contribute an equal amount to match the grant. As an example, if you apply for £1,500 in grant funding to buy a new computer system, you must be able to contribute a further £1,500 towards purchasing the computer system, meaning the total purchase would be £3,000.

Coverage: Adur and Worthing Borough, West Sussex.

Business Grant

In collaboration with the local enterprise and apprenticeship platform, Arun Valley Borough Council are providing grants for new businesses who need to fund their starting up, as well as more established small businesses who can achieve a meaningful objective by gaining grant funding.

Funding: the grant is up to £2,000 per business and is for companies located in the Arun Valley area. They also have free start-up courses and business start-up workshops available in Bognor Regis.
Coverage: Arun District, West Sussex.

Chichester District Council Grant Programme

The Chichester District Council Grant Programme is designed to support small businesses and economic growth within the Chichester District. As such, there are two types of grant funding. The first, 'Fast track', is a quicker, less intensive application process for grants of under £1,000. Above this is a general grants programme for grants of more than £1,000.

To be eligible for a grant, you have to meet the three priorities of the council's grant funding agenda and the six principles of any project (information available at   http://www.chichester.gov.uk/article/24752/ Chichester-District-Council-grant-programme). You will need to contact a funding advisor at Chichester District Council in order to apply.

Funding: you can apply for financing below £1,000 and also above to a maximum not stipulated.
Coverage: Chichester District, West Sussex.

Business Support Grants

Crawley Borough Council runs a grant scheme to provide start-ups and small businesses with initial funding to help them get off the ground or expand in the early years. You can apply using the council application form. Grant applications are reviewed every four weeks until funds run out.

Funding: up to £2,000, the grant must be match funded up to 50% of the project cost.
Coverage: Crawley Borough, West Sussex.

East Sussex Invest 5 (ESI5)

An RGF-funded grants scheme, East Sussex Invest 5 is run by East Sussex County Council and Locate East Sussex. The grant is intended to stimulate economic growth and job creation by supporting small businesses to grow. There appear to be no criteria apart from being a small business in the area.

Funding: between £15,000 and £40,000 is available, requiring match funding of 60% of the total amount. There is also an option for loan finance of £10,000 to £200,000. This, too, involves match funding up to 50% and may incur an administration fee of £500.

Coverage: East Sussex.

Scheme Enabling Fund (SEF)

SEF is a substantial fund dedicated to supporting developers in carrying out finance feasibility studies and business case development of new housing schemes, and in restarting stalled housing schemes to generate employment and housing. To apply for this fund, you will need to contact the economic intervention team at East Sussex County Council.

Funding: the maximum amount to be considered is not listed, but the remaining fund size is £600,000. The fund will close once it's exhausted.

Coverage: East Sussex.

Digital Skills for Growth (DSG)

The DSG is run by the Essex Employment and Skills Board. It offers businesses in the Essex area grants for training young people aged 19 to 24 in digital technologies. The grant is listed on the council website.

Funding: up to £4,000.

Coverage: Essex.

Small Grants Scheme

Set up and run by the New Anglia Local Enterprise Partnership, the Small Grants Scheme exists to support businesses. The grant is available for businesses wanting to expand or grow, build services or products or gain greater efficiencies or productivity. Any company must be located in specific parts of Norfolk and Suffolk. Application forms are available on the New Anglia Growth Hub website.

Funding: the grant is between £1,000 and £25,000 and will pay for up to 20% of the total cost of any project. Nearly £900,000 has been allocated so far to over 95 different projects put forward by businesses.

Coverage: Norfolk and Suffolk.

Growing Business Fund

The Growing Business Fund is a larger version of the Small Grants Scheme offered by New Anglia, with slightly different criteria. It is designed to support more established businesses who are looking to grow, to invest, to recruit or expand. The Growing Business Fund is in partnership with New Anglia LEP, Finance East and Suffolk County Council.

Funding: the grant provides up to £500,000 in funding and covers a maximum of 20% of the overall cost of a project. For example, if you apply for £400,000, you will need to come up with the further £1.6 million to cover a £2 million project.

Coverage: Norfolk and Suffolk.

Start-Up Grant

The Start-Up Grant is an initiative from Broadland District Council to support unemployed people commencing a business. The main criteria are that you can only apply after a period of unemployment, your new business must be your full-time profession, and you will need to provide a reliable business plan and cash flow projection. You can register a profile and apply online. If successful, the grant will be paid once your business begins trading.

Funding: up to £750.

Coverage: Broadland District, Norfolk.

Enterprise Grant

A funding initiative from Broadland District Council aimed firmly at existing small businesses who need the funding to expand. To be eligible for the grant, you will need to have fewer than ten staff and be based in the Broadland District. You will also be required to submit your business's accounts, and quotes for the equipment or work you plan to pay for with the grant to expand your business.

Funding: up to £750.

Coverage: Broadland District, Norfolk.

Scale up Coaching Grants

Business West in collaboration with the European Union Development Fund is providing scale up coaching grants to businesses for them to hire business coaches to advise them in scaling their enterprises. All SMEs in the West of England who are looking to grow in the next 12 months or create jobs are eligible for this scheme.

You can meet the Business West Enterprise team to chat more about the grant and funding possibilities at the Engine Shed in Bristol before making an application.

Funding: £1,000 to £2,500. The grant can cover a maximum of 40% of total project/hiring a coach expenses.

Coverage: West of England.

The Gloucester Business Growth Grant Scheme

Gloucester City Council manages this grant scheme, with the objective of supporting local economic growth by providing grants to businesses located in Gloucester. The grant must be used towards capital costs, such as premises or equipment purchases among others.

You must express interest through completing a form (expression of interest form available on the council's website) and, once assessed/ approved for grant funding, provide the receipts. You will then be reimbursed for the project. (You will need to be able to pay the full amount up front, which seems odd given it's match funded!)

Funding: £1,000 to £10,000, with most grants limited to £5,000. The grant can represent 30% of total project costs for businesses outside the city centre and 50% of total expenses for businesses inside the city centre.

Coverage: Forest of Dean, Gloucestershire.

Malvern Hills Business Start-Up Grant

Malvern Hills Council runs a grant scheme to support businesses based in the district. The aim behind the scheme is to fill vacant business premises, regenerate town centres and create new jobs. Therefore you must be able to demonstrate how your business or project will achieve this.

To be eligible, you need to be employed full time by your business, provide a business plan and have the relevant business licences to operate in place.

Funding: a maximum of £750 can be applied for. This reduces to £500 if you're not moving into a rateable business property.

Coverage: Malvern Hills District Council, Worcestershire County.

Investment Fund

The Investment Fund is run by Coventry City Council in collaboration with Warwickshire County Council and Coventry University Enterprises. The grant is to help small and well-established businesses in need of financial support to start or grow.

The scheme is specifically for businesses with less than 250 employees that are looking to invest in capital assets such as computer hardware, software, machinery, new premises and much more. You must also not have received a grant previously from the council and be able to show the need for the grant for your business. To apply, contact one of the business development advisors at the council to start the process and guide you through.

Funding: the grant will cover 30% of the cost of a project, with a maximum project contribution of between £1,000 and £50,000.

Coverage: Warwickshire.

Innovation Programme

The Innovation Programme is designed to support small and medium-sized businesses developing or looking to create innovative services or products.

Regarding criteria, they are specifically looking for companies involved in developing emerging technologies in the areas of energy, data, IT connectivity, IOT, assistive technologies, advanced materials and more. These areas are not definitive so it is likely your business will be applicable if you are developing new or early development technologies. To be suitable, you must also have less than 250 employees. You can apply by speaking to the innovation team at Coventry City Council.

Funding: not currently indicated but, given the enthusiasm of the grant listing page and Coventry's historical support of innovation and internationally patented technologies, it will likely be substantial.

Coverage: Warwickshire.

Energy Efficiency Grants

As part of the council's Green Energy programme, the Energy Efficiency Grants scheme provides sizable grants to businesses looking to increase their energy efficiency through the introduction and acquisition of equipment that will lead to overall energy consumption reduction and carbon savings for a business.

Funding: between £1,000 and £50,000, the grant can cover a maximum 30% of overall costs towards energy efficiency measures.

Coverage: Warwickshire.

Low Carbon Innovation Grants

This scheme provides financial support for businesses developing or investing in low carbon technology. The grant can cover costs related to technology development for nuclear energy, offshore wind, waste processing, recycling, and energy efficient doors, fittings and fixtures, as examples.

Funding: £1,000 to £50,000, the grant covers 30% of development capital costs.

Coverage: Warwickshire.

Low Carbon Revenue Grants

This scheme provides grant funding for businesses seeking to commercialise products in the low carbon market, including those that are new to a market or new to the company applying for the grant.

Funding: the grant provides a maximum of £6,000 in funding and can cover up to 40% of revenue-related costs, i.e. software, consultancy, market research or prototype development.

Coverage: Warwickshire.

Warwickshire County Council Growth Fund

Warwickshire County Council has a £2,000,000 fund to support businesses in the Warwickshire area, with a focus on micro and small businesses for capital-based projects and expenditures. Applicants must be able to show tremendous growth potential from the use of the grant.

Priority is given to businesses in sectors including tourism, low carbon tech, creative industries, digital media, among other areas.

Funding: the grant can cover £5,000 to £35,000 and up to 40% of total project costs. (Loan finance is also available from £1,000 to £50,000.)

Coverage: North Warwickshire.

Business Support Programme

A dual-stream grants programme catering for businesses with small capital and substantial capital needs, the schemes are designed to support enterprise in the Coventry and Warwickshire area. For more information related to acceptable costs and further criteria, you will need to contact the council.

Funding: small businesses, £1,000 to £10,000. Large businesses in priority areas can access up to £50,000. Rates on grants vary, depending on business size and location, from 10% to 30%.

Coverage: Coventry and Warwickshire.

Northamptonshire Digital Enhancement Programme

The Digital Enhancement Programme provides financing to support SMEs in digitally enhancing their business in some way. This could take the form of creating an e-commerce website, upgrading an ordering system, developing bespoke software in-house or a new digital product or application to support the business's operation.

To be eligible you need to have a company based in Northamptonshire, be a small to medium enterprise with less than 250 people, and have a clear plan and idea of how new technologies and capabilities gained as a result of the grant will help your business.

Funding: up to £5,000, 50% match funded.

Coverage: Northamptonshire.

Ready2Grow

With £220,000+ in grant funding already given out, the Ready2Grow funding scheme is an excellent source of finance for new and expanding businesses based in Northamptonshire that are looking for financial and informational support and advice to achieve and sustain growth.

To apply, you will need to reach out to the council and propose a relevant project within your business. They will then be able to advise you. The total process will likely take eight to 12 weeks.

Funding: the grant total is based on the amount the council business advisor deems right.

Coverage: Northamptonshire.

Grants and funding

Rutland County Council offer different types of financial support to new and small businesses choosing to call Rutland County home. These grants are match funded and designed to support a wide range of business applications, depending on location and business size.

Funding: you will need to contact the economic development team for exact numbers.

Coverage: Rutland County.

Growing Enterprise – Grant for Enterprise

A grant programme to support the growth and diversification of SMEs in the Lincolnshire area, this is for both capital and revenue projects.

Funding: between £1,000 and £2,000 covering 25% of total costs.

Coverage: Lincolnshire County.

Greater Lincolnshire Growth Fund

The Growth Fund is a large grant fund of nearly £3,000,000 open for businesses operating in a few core areas, including low carbon, digital, healthcare, visitor economy and agri-food.

Proposed projects and businesses must be able to show a positive impact on the local economy through their enterprises. To be eligible for a grant of £150,000, you will need to create at least 27 jobs, and at least 90 jobs for a grant of £500,000. The grant can be spent on costs including building new infrastructure, machinery, equipment, recruitment, staff and modern technology.

Funding: the grant ranges between £150,000 and £500,000. For small and micro businesses with up to 50 employees, 30% of the total project cost will be covered by the grant. For more extensive businesses with 51 employees or more, the grant will cover 20% of the total cost.

Coverage: Lincolnshire County.

Growing Graduate Enterprise

Growth Lincolnshire is a scheme from the University of Lincolnshire that offers a monetary grant and support to final year university students in Lincolnshire who plan to stay in the county and start a new business.

To be eligible, your business cannot be trading, you must live in the Lincolnshire area, have no visa restrictions and have a viable business idea.

Funding: £2,500 (split into two principal payments of £1,500 and £1,000).

Coverage: Lincolnshire County.

Business Growth and Digital Growth Grants (GLLEP – Greater Lincolnshire Local Enterprise Partnership)

The Business Growth and Digital Growth Grants support businesses purchasing equipment, software, e-commerce solutions and digital management systems.

If your business can demonstrate that a grant investment will help you to significantly increase your turnover or create new jobs in the Lincolnshire area, you will also need to speak with a Business Lincolnshire advisor to agree your plan and activities before any grant authorisation.

Funding: £1,000 to £10,000 and between 30% to 50% of total cost.

Coverage: Lincolnshire County.

Innovation Programme for Greater Lincolnshire

The Innovation Grant Programme offers access to proof of concept grants and innovation vouchers. The initial grant provides funds for SMEs to build new products and processes or create new markets. The second grant provides funding for SMEs to hire consultants to carry out research and consultancy for technological and innovation projects.

Funding: proof of concept grants are between £1,000 and £10,000. Innovation vouchers are from £1,000 to £5,000.

Coverage: Lincolnshire County.

Grants4Growth

A capital funding grant designed to support business growth. Eligible businesses in the South Holland area can use the grant to fund the purchase of capital assets needed to increase sales, production, create innovations or drive efficiencies, ultimately contributing to local economic growth and job creation.

The application process is incredibly quick, with the council aiming to get a decision to you within two weeks.

Funding: from £1,000 to £25,000 up to 28% of the cost of any capital purchase can be paid for by the grant.

Coverage: South Holland, Lincolnshire.

Business Start-Up Grant

Offered by Mansfield District Council, the Business Start-Up Grant is available for applications from all residents in the Mansfield area. The grant can be used to fund the costs of starting up. Start-up costs can include purchasing equipment, advertising, building a website and more.

Funding: up to £1,000.

Coverage: Mansfield District, Nottinghamshire.

Ashfield Markets Grant

The Ashfield Markets Grant allows new market traders to get a financial grant to support their new venture in moving into the Idlewells Indoor Market.

Funding: up to £1,500. It also provides up to £500 for traders looking to move into several local indoor markets.

Coverage: Mansfield District, Nottinghamshire.

Mansfield Market Grant

The Mansfield Market Grant provides up to 12 months of market stall rent. The programme aims to support new market traders and provide representation at the market of under-represented products.

Funding: up to 12 months rent-free at the market.

Coverage: Mansfield District, Nottinghamshire.

Business Growth Grant

This Business Growth Grant is for slightly more established businesses who can produce a solid business plan and create at least one full-time job as a result of the project and grant. The Mansfield team will also help you form a growth plan and calculate the costs involved.

Funding: up to £5,000.

Coverage: Mansfield District, Nottinghamshire.

Business Start-Up Grant Scheme

A start-up grant from Cheshire West and Cheshire Council to support residents in launching new businesses or enterprises. This includes new ventures not older than three months.

To apply, you will need to supply details of a business advisor and an updated business plan and cash flow forecast. You must also prove the grant is necessary to start up your business.

Funding: grant funding available is a maximum of £250.

Coverage: Cheshire West and Chester.

The Rochdale Apprenticeship Progression Grant

The Apprenticeship Progression Grant is run by the Rochdale Borough Council and can provide employers with a grant for further educating apprentices. This grant also provides funding for the apprentice. The priority for funding is in the areas of management, engineering, manufacturing and health and social care.

The funding is issued when apprentices progress to advanced or higher apprenticeship qualifications in priority sectors and are residents of Rochdale.

Funding: £1,000 per apprentice with a maximum of two grants per employer.

Coverage: Rochdale Metropolitan Borough, Greater Manchester.

Regional Investment Aid Merseyside

This is a fund designed to alleviate unemployment in Merseyside and provide money and jobs by giving grant funding to small, medium and large enterprises. Any grant can be used for construction, paying staff or buying/replacing machinery and equipment.

Businesses from all types of industries are welcome to apply, apart from those in steel, synthetic fibres, coal, shipbuilding, fisheries, or agriculture product production.

Funding: not stipulated but pinned to the intervention rate set for SMEs and large businesses by the regional aid map of 2013.

Coverage: Liverpool City, Merseyside.

Regenerus Start-Up Grant

The Regenerus Start-Up Grant is available to new businesses situated in the Merseyside region. The director of the fund is Regenerus, previously known as South Sefton Development Trust. The programme includes a combination of workshops and one-on-one assistance from a qualified business advisor to produce your business plan and cash flow forecasts.

To be eligible, you must be based in Merseyside. Application details are provided on the Regenerus website.

Funding: a start-up grant of £250.

Coverage: Merseyside.

Starting in Business Grant

A micro grant to support entrepreneurs in the Chorley area to turn their business ideas into new businesses. To apply, you will need to contact a business advisor at Chorley Council.

Funding: up to £750. This can be in the form of a traditional grant or a loan.

Coverage: Chorley, Lancashire.

Shop Front Improvement Grant

Run by Chorley Council, the Shop Front Improvement Grant is a grant scheme for local retailers who wish to improve the visual exterior of vacant/occupied retail properties. To be eligible, you must be a leaseholder or owner of a retail property in Chorley town centre.

Funding: up to 75% of the project costs to a maximum of £10,000.

Coverage: Chorley, Lancashire.

Business Investment for Growth Grant (BIG)

The BIG grant is for businesses in the Chorley area that wish to expand and, in the process, will create jobs and make capital expenditures. Expenses the grant can cover include renovation/building of business premises, security improvements and other costs.

You can apply by submitting an application form on the council website.

Funding: 50% of the project costs to a maximum of £10,000, with grants being administered in the order of £2,000 for each job created.

Coverage: Chorley, Lancashire.

Chorley Relocation Grant

Businesses that choose to relocate permanently to Chorley and bring at least 20 long-term jobs to the area within 18 months of relocating may apply for what is a quite sizable grant and incentive to relocate a business.

The above are the only criteria, the limitation being that retail businesses cannot apply for this small business grant.

Funding: up to £25,000, with £1,250 being provided per job brought.

Coverage: Chorley, Lancashire.

Grants for Growing and Developing Your Business

A funding and finance scheme for private sector businesses based in Pendle that are looking to build and expand their operations in the borough, the grant is designed to support growth initiatives and overall job creation with economic benefit generation.

To be eligible, your business must be over six months old and be paying small business rates in Pendle. To start the grant application process, you will need to arrange an initial site visit from a council advisor before you complete the application form.

Funding: £2,000 to £10,000, grants can cover up to 25% of total project costs.

Coverage: Pendle Borough, Lancashire.

Regenerate Pennine Lancashire

The Ribble Valley Borough Council are providing grants for entrepreneurs with new businesses, or those who have recently started, with their partner, Regenerate. They also offer access to free coaching, workshops and more.

To apply, you will need to contact the Hyndburn Enterprise Trust.

Funding: not stipulated. (The inference is that funding is partial; assume match funding requirement.)

Coverage: Ribble Valley Borough, Lancashire.

Business Network Support Fund

Initiated in 2014 by Hambleton District Council, the Business Network Support Fund is part of an economic strategy to support business networks in the Hambleton area in combining and growing.

The grant funding can be spent on working to increase network membership, marketing or communicating to new or existing target audiences, and developing links with other networks. You can apply via an online application form but you must be a developing or established business network in the Hambleton area.

Funding: up to £4,000. However, for grants over a £1,000, the council would expect at least a 20% contribution to the application project by the recipient.

Coverage: Hambleton District, Yorkshire.

Business Start-Up Grants

A small grant provided by the Scarborough Borough Council to support start-up businesses less than 18 months old. Applications for the grant can be made to purchase equipment and machinery, improvement of premises and different types of marketing.

Funding: up to £1,000 for one business in one year.

Coverage: Scarborough Borough, Yorkshire.

Business Expansion Grants

The Business Expansion Grants are designed to support existing businesses in Scarborough Borough to expand and consolidate their market position, or expand into new markets. The grants are intended to help fund actively revenue-generating projects as opposed to covering capital expenses.

Funding: up to £5,000 for one business in one year.

Coverage: Scarborough Borough, Yorkshire.

Business Development Grant Scheme

The Business Development Start-Up Grant Scheme has been established to encourage the formation of new businesses in Scarborough Borough. The director of the funds is Scarborough Borough Council. Start-up grants are targeted at new start-ups and companies less than 18 months old. An application can be made for assistance towards the cost of necessary equipment and machinery.

Funding: the amount of funding available is £1 to £1,000. Any grant awarded will be 50% of expenditure within the limits of the grant amount.

Coverage: Scarborough, North Yorkshire.

Hartlepool Business Grants

Hartlepool Council offers a range of business grants to support local businesses. However, they do not provide information about these grants on their website but ask you to contact their enterprise team for more details.

They say that grants will cover areas including accessing international markets, development of information technology, employment creation and more.

Funding: not stipulated.

Coverage: Hartlepool Borough, Durham.

Stockton Town Centre Retail Grant

To support the revival of Stockton Town Centre, the local council are offering retail businesses a sizable grant towards commercial building rental. For new businesses, the grant will cover renting a vacant property; for existing businesses, it could cover extra floor space or premises rented necessary to expand and support growth.

Funding: £5,000 (in some cases this can be increased to £10,000).

Coverage: Stockton-On-Tees, Durham.

Social Impact Investment Fund Grant Scheme

In collaboration with Sellafield Ltd, Allerdale Borough Council has set up a social impact fund, one of the primary purposes being to provide funding and grants to support and grow start-ups and small businesses in the Allerdale area.

The scheme is focused on grassroots small businesses or new ventures that can have a positive social or economic impact. Further to this, any applicant to the grant scheme must demonstrate they have faith in their business venture by having put finance into their business previously or having raised it from an external finance source, i.e. investment, bank or loan. If you are looking for low-cost loan finance, they also provide loans for more substantial amounts and presumably competitive rates compared to traditional lenders.

Funding: the grant is administered annually and no specific funding amount is detailed. You will need to fill out an expression of interest form to find out more.

Coverage: Allerdale Borough, Cumbria.

Shop Front Grant Scheme

Launched in 2014 by Barrow Borough Council, the Shop Front Grant Scheme has funding of £120,000 and provides grants for businesses on specific streets in Barrow Town Centre that are looking to renovate or upgrade their shop fronts. For example, this could include new windows, facias, signage or lighting. The grant is for small retailers and small independent businesses with less than 50 employees.

Furthermore, to be eligible for the grant, you must be enhancing the property in some way, not carrying out maintenance. Your business must also be open five days a week, must occupy the unit/building proposed for renovation, and have property ownership or tenancy for a minimum of 12 months. In addition, projects must be professionally designed, cover only exterior finish, and you cannot have successfully applied for a previous Shop Front Grant from the 2010 or 2012 scheme.

It's also worth noting that, if you sell the property that uses the grant or the business closes within two years, a certain percentage of the grant must be repaid depending on the time elapsed.

Funding: the grant size applied for can vary but the grant can only fund 75% of any renovations or work. The owner/grant applicant must provide the further 25%.

Coverage: Barrow-in-Furness Borough, Cumbria.

Cumbria Business Start-Up Support Programme

The fund director is the Cumbria Chamber of Commerce. You should not have more than 250 employees involved in your business and there is a telephone-based application to assess your eligibility. You can apply through the Cumbria Chamber website.

Funding: the Business Start-Up Support Programme (BSUS) offers free business advice, support and training to anyone looking to start a new business or set up a social enterprise, or those in the first three years of trading. There's also business support offered to women based in rural Cumbria. The business training course focuses on areas such as social media marketing and search engine optimisation.

Coverage: Cumbria.

Power To Change Funding

In collaboration with Collaborate CIC, the Power To Change funding programme is there to provide financial and informational support to community businesses based in Suffolk. The grant is for community-oriented businesses in the idea, planning or early running stages.

There are three main programmes:

» The £1.85 million Community Business Bright Ideas Fund is aimed at community groups who have a community business idea but need help turning it into reality.

» The Community Business Trade Up Programme is for early stage community businesses that are planning to grow.

»   The £10 million Community Business Fund is aimed at existing community businesses that need funding for a business development project to make their organisation more sustainable.

More details can be found on the Power To Change website.

To be eligible, you must be starting or running a community business. In the eyes of Suffolk County Council, this means being locally based, addressing community needs, being accountable to the local community, and having a trading model that benefits the community and has an overall broad, positive impact on the community as a whole.

Funding: £250 to £5,000 (funding dependent on the stage and type of project).

Coverage: nationwide.

Evalu8 Low Carbon Transport

Under the Innovation Grants scheme, Evalu8 are actively offering consultancy on low carbon transport technology to SMEs in the East of England.

The grant is intended for companies who need advice on developing new products, services or processes related to low carbon transport technology. There are no specific eligibility requirements beyond what's required under the Innovation Voucher Scheme.

Funding: £1,000 worth of consultancy.

Coverage: Herefordshire, Cambridgeshire, Suffolk, Norfolk and Bedfordshire.

HS2 Supply Chain Programme (High Speed 2)

As part of the £33,000,000 Business Growth Programme, the High Speed 2 Supply Chain Programme is working with four Local Enterprise Partnerships (LEPs) in the Midlands area to support businesses that have, or have the ability to secure, a commercial contract for HS2.

To be eligible, your business must meet the criteria above, purely operate in B2B sector, and be based in areas belonging to one of the four LEPs.

Funding: from £20,000 to £167,000 available per project. The grant can cover between 10% and 50% of the overall cost.

Coverage: Birmingham City Council, The Marches, Stoke-on-Trent, and Staffordshire and Greater Birmingham and Solihull.

Food Processing Grants

From a combination of multiple government departments, the Food Processing Grants Scheme is funded by the European Agricultural Fund for Rural Development.

The scheme endeavours to support businesses making capital investments to create a new company or grow within a rural area. This programme aims to develop the rural economy and generate sustainable employment in the countryside. You will find full programme details under the RDPE Growth Programme documentation (there are significant requirements to be eligible for grants).

Funding: minimum grant size of £35,000 is typical.

Coverage: North East, North West, Midlands, Yorkshire and Humber, East Midlands, South East and South West.

NBV Grant for New Businesses

The NBV Business Grant is for businesses based in Nottinghamshire, Derbyshire, Leicestershire and Greater Lincolnshire. Your business needs to be B2B and ready to start trading. It also has to be already registered with HMRC or Companies House. You need to start by expressing your interest on the NBV website.

Funding: the grant amount can be anywhere from £1,000 to £2,500 depending on the project spend.

Coverage: Nottinghamshire, Derbyshire, Leicestershire and Greater Lincolnshire.

Built Environment Climate Change Innovations (BECCI)

This BECCI scheme is administered by multiple councils, local authorities and universities. It is a European funded project across the UK designed to promote economic growth and opportunities for small and medium-sized businesses to create climate change solutions and technologies.

If you're evolving climate change technologies and solutions and require further development, testing or want to showcase a product you already have, your business could benefit from a BECCI grant.

Funding: one body has over £1,000,000 available for the project, and amounts vary project to project. It is worth consulting with a delivery body in your area to see what the numbers could be, but assume substantial.

Coverage: Coventry and Wolverhampton University, Hartlepool Borough, Durham.

Business Energy Efficiency Programme (BEEP)

The BEEP grants are administered by multiple bodies and are available for businesses looking to use energy more efficiently and get better environmental credentials. To be eligible, you need to employ fewer than 250 people and have a turnover of under £40,000,000.

Funding: £2,000 to £20,000.

Coverage: Worcestershire County, Hartlepool Borough, Durham.

Wales

Start-Up Business Grants

Available to start-up businesses up to a year old, the Start-up Business Grant from UK Steel Enterprise and Newport City Council is designed to provide funding support to pre-start-ups and relatively new businesses that will grow the local economy and create jobs. You can use the grant to pay for costs including software, training, commercial rent and more.

Awarding of the grant is discretionary and carried out by the council. Social enterprises, companies, sole traders, and all organisations are eligible to apply.

Funding: up to £1,500. The grant funding is up to 40% of the total cost of any project.

Coverage: Newport City.

Vacant Commercial Floor Space Grant

From Newport City Council, this grant is for businesses who rent new commercial premises in the city centre or take on additional floor space for their business. The grant will cover the first year's rent on any property.

To be eligible, your business must be based in Newport town centre, or you must be planning to base your business there. You must have paid all business rates to date, have a business plan, cashflow forecast and one year's profit and loss accounts. The amount of grant funding provided is based on sources of finance an applicant has open to them.

Funding: 50% match funding to a maximum of £6,000 – i.e. if you apply for £6,000, you will need to have £6,000 to invest if successful in applying for a grant.

Coverage: Newport City.

Business Development Grant

Run by the Caerphilly County Borough Council, the Business Development Grant is for small businesses in, or supplying to, the manufacturing industry, or that have over 60% of their business as B2B. The grant covers purchasing new equipment or services that must improve the business, i.e. capital equipment, websites and e-commerce, business planning, marketing and feasibility studies.

To apply, you will need to provide profit and loss statements, cash flow projections and a business plan, plus management accounts for the last two years if you're trading and your business is older than six months. You will also need to provide a minimum of two quotes for anything you plan to purchase with the grant. You can apply by reaching out to the business enterprise support team for the council.

Funding: this is a discretionary grant up to £2,000 and can pay for up to 45% of the cost of the new equipment or services provided.

Coverage: Caerphilly County.

Business Start-Up Grant

This is funding from UK Steel Enterprise in conjunction with Caerphilly County Council in the form of micro business grants to help residents in Caerphilly set up a business for the first time. The council requires that the grant funding is used for purchasing building works, marketing, development of a website or capital/IT equipment.

To apply, you will need to supply a business plan of cash flow and profit/loss projections for at least one year. You will also need to provide two quotes for any proposed purchases under the grant, and at least one of the company directors must be employed by the company full time.

Funding: the grant funds project costs up to £500 and must be 50% match funded – i.e. if you apply for £500 you will need a further £500 to put in yourself.

Coverage: Caerphilly County.

Commercial Improvement Grants

This grant is for tenants or owners of business properties in Caerphilly County whose buildings have become run down over time and could benefit from renovation. These renovations include exterior landscaping, improvements to physical infrastructure, extension or development of commercial or retail buildings.

To successfully apply for the Commercial Improvement Grant, you need to show how your project can create additional jobs, keep existing jobs, achieve environmental improvement, bring vacant properties into use, and enhance and improve the local street environment where your business premises is situated. This grant is typically used by retail shop owners but is not limited in this respect. As such, it could apply to other areas, including office spaces in the right conditions.

You will need to fill in an expression of interest form to begin the grant application process. Once past that stage, you'll then need to provide an application based on the council specification.

Funding: provides up to 50% of the costs of any work to a maximum of £15,000 for a single property.

Coverage: Caerphilly County.

B2B / Start-Up Grants

Business Development Grant Caerphilly

This grant is aimed at businesses that are looking to grow in Caerphilly. The maximum number of employees should be 250 or less. The director of the grant is Caerphilly County Borough Council. The business must be a full-time operation and be established in Caerphilly, and at least one of the owners or directors must be involved in the business full time.

Funding: the maximum amount of funding available is £2,000.

Coverage: Caerphilly.

Enterprise Support Programme

The Enterprise Support Programme provides funding and assistance to existing and new private companies/social enterprises in the Rhondda Cynon Taf area. This grant can contribute towards the purchase of capital equipment, including information technology, improvement to business premises, website coding and more.

Funding levels vary (details below), but to qualify for up to £5,000 you must be creating one new full-time job, and for up to £10,000 you must be creating two full-time jobs. You will need to complete an expression of interest form to apply.

Funding: start-ups that have been trading for under 12 months can get between £500 and £10,000 in funding, with a maximum of 40% of project cost being provided by the grant. Existing businesses older than one year can apply for between £1,000 and £10,000, with a maximum grant contribution of 40% towards total cost. Home-based businesses can apply for a maximum grant of £1,500.

Coverage: Rhondda Cynon Taf.

Vibrant and Viable Places Business Retail Funding

Funded by the Welsh government, the Vibrant and Viable grant scheme supports retail businesses in the centre of Merthyr Tydfil. The funding can be used for the purchase of equipment, ICT and other hardware. To discuss applying, contact the Economic Development Team.

Funding: £500 to £5,000. Up to 70% of project costs are covered.

Coverage: Merthyr Tydfil County.

BG Kick Start Grant Scheme

A combined grant funding initiative from the UK Steel Enterprise fund and Blaenau Gwent County Borough Council regeneration division, the Kick Start Grant Scheme is designed to support small businesses and new ventures. The only criteria for applicants seem to be that your project must be a start-up in the Blaenau Gwent area. You can apply by contacting the council's economic development team.

Funding: the grant has to be 50% match funded and the maximum amount of funding provided is £2,000. For example, to apply for £2,000, you will need £2,000 of your own money to invest in the business.

Coverage: Blaenau Gwent County.

BG Effect Business Fund

Very similar to the BG Kick Start Scheme above and with the same application criteria, the BG Effect Business Fund is there to support start-up businesses in the Blaenau Gwent area.

Funding: 80% of the total funding for any project up to the amount of £2,000. You can also get free expert advice and support from your local enterprise network.

Coverage: Blaenau Gwent County.

Community Toilet Grant Scheme

Recently launched by the Gwynedd County Council, the Toilet Grant Scheme offers a one-off small grant to businesses who provide their toilets for public use in the Gwynedd area. This is to improve the range of facilities available to the public in the town centre.

Funding: one-off payment of £500.

Coverage: Gwynedd County.

ISO Grant Scheme

The ISO Grant Scheme aims to help local businesses to achieve ISO accreditations. The grant is a monetary contribution towards the cost of consultant fees necessary to meet the correct standard for certification.

Funding: not stipulated.

Coverage: Gwynedd County.

ReAct for Businesses

ReAct is a grant fund programme from the Welsh Assembly Government with two primary funding initiatives for businesses in the Flintshire area. The first grant scheme is the Employer Recruitment Support Fund which supports employers/small businesses that recruit individuals made redundant in the previous six months. The second scheme is the Employer Training Support Grant. This provides a fund that employers can put towards training recruits in job-related skills. You will need to contact the ReAct team for more details and to apply via phone.

Funding: for the Employer Recruitment Support Fund, the grant is up to £2,080, paid in four instalments. For the Employer Training Support Grant, up to a £1,000 is available per business.

Coverage: Flintshire County.

Scotland

Start-Up Grant West Dunbartonshire

The Start-Up Grant is reserved for people looking to launch their own business. The director of the grant is West Dunbartonshire Council and the maximum number of employees you should have to be eligible is 250. A business plan, as well as proof of trading, must be provided to qualify. You can enquire about the grant from the details provided on the West Dunbartonshire website.

Funding: a grant of £500 is available to help people over 18 with costs of starting a business.

Coverage: West Dunbartonshire.

FIFE Investment Fund

The director of this fund is Business Gateway Fife, and the grant specifically focuses on small businesses. You should not have more than 49 employees and must be based in Fife. You will be given preference if you are working in creative or environmental industries, or a B2B market. You can find application details on Fife's website.

Funding: you can receive a grant of between £5,000 and £20,000. Business Gateway Fife administers funds on behalf of Fife Council. A business review and a fully functional business plan must be a part of any application.

Coverage: Fife.

Grants for New Businesses in Orkney

These grants are available to people who are looking to start a new business in the Orkney region, and are managed by the Orkney Business Gateway. An application company should comprise no more than nine employees, and applicants for start-up funding must be developing a new, full-time business. A business plan and two years of cash flow projections must be submitted, and the business must not be launched before the application submission. The grant may cover any start-up costs, such as equipment, training and marketing. For more information, you can contact the Orkney Business Gateway via their website.

Funding: the maximum amount provided is £1,000.

Coverage: Orkney Island.

New Business Grants

This list covers a range of national and regional business grants meant explicitly for those starting a new business or venture that is in idea stage, has just been set up and, in some cases, that has been running for a short period of time. These small business grants are typically less but easier to apply for and successfully get funding from.

Prince's Trust Grants

The Prince's Trust Grants have been dedicated to rendering financial assistance to young entrepreneurs since 1976. The Trust offers an exclusive Enterprise Programme that provides grants and mentors to young individuals to help them start their own businesses. To apply for the grant, you must be between 18 and 30 years old and are required to fill in the online application form.

Funding: for individuals, the grant offered is £1,500, whereas a business group may access a grant of up to £3,000. A test marketing grant of up to £250 is also provided to individuals, to help them evaluate the market value of their product.

Heritage Lottery Fund Start-Up Grants

Heritage Lottery Grants are only offered to individuals running a non-profit organisation, or entrepreneurs who are going to start a new business. They can also help entrepreneurs with introducing new set-ups for their businesses. The Heritage Lottery Fund takes the outcomes of your business endeavours into consideration when assessing applications, which remain open for the whole year so you can apply at any time. It takes eight months to process the application.

Funding: no amount is specified but it does depend on the state of your business.

Childcare Business Grants Scheme

A recently-opened grants programme, the Childcare Business Grants Scheme is intended to support entrepreneurs in setting up their own childcare business. This grant programme is part of the UK government's strategy to increase the amount of childcare available to UK working parents while decreasing the overall cost.

Only new businesses are eligible to apply for this grant. This means they must not be more than three months old and they must have been registered after 1 May 2017. Grants are available for three specific types of business:

» Early years' childcare provider or childminder on domestic premises.

» Early years' childcare provider or childminder working with special needs or disabled children on domestic premises.

» A standard childminder agency.

The scheme is from the Department of Education. There is a limited amount of funding available, and the scheme will stop once this fund has expired, so apply soon!

Funding: grants of £500 or £1,000 are available.

New Enterprise Allowance

The New Enterprise Allowance is a grant fund dedicated to supporting unemployed people with becoming self-employed and running their own business. The scheme provides a grant in the form of a weekly allowance over a 26-week period. You are likely to be eligible if you or your partner are receiving any benefits (JSA, UC or SA).

Aside from a monetary grant, you will also receive a mentor to provide guidance and support through planning, setting up and running your new business. If you have been out of work for a while, this scheme is perfect for helping you to set up an enterprise. You can find out more about the scheme by going to your local Jobcentre Plus and speaking to a work coach.

Funding: a weekly allowance worth up to £1,274 over a 26-week period.

The Environment Now

In partnership with O2, the National Youth Agency is running The Environment Now, a programme that provides grants to young people (aged 17 to 24) who have come up with or are exploring inventive ways to use digital technology to provide innovative solutions to environmental issues.

The grant is primarily for young people innovating in improving energy efficiency, recycling and reducing waste. In addition to a grant, you will receive work experience, mentoring and professional insight into your project area.

Funding: up to £10,000.

That concludes the round-up of grants available. As you can see, there is money out there to support you in your venture if you know where to look. However, whilst correct at the time of going to press, this is probably not a comprehensive list and will certainly be subject to ongoing change. Funding Nav tries to stay abreast of these changes and can advise on any current opportunities should you be in the market for grant funding.

Other Ways of Getting Free Cash

Asset utilisation

You know the feeling of finding a pound coin under the cushion of your sofa, or a forgotten ten pound note in a pair of trousers you haven't worn for some time? Well, that's the idea behind this strategy that is always one of the first things Funding Nav looks at when we come into a new client's business.

Businesses don't grow in straight lines, do they? Generally, they create demand and then increase their capacity so that they can match it with their supply. But often, supply moves ahead of demand because you generally can't increase your facilities, such as office or warehouse space, in a smooth, straight line, as the cost and inconvenience of change is too high. So, businesses can run with surplus capacity of space, desks, human resources, distribution or delivery.

Alternatively, even when a business claims to be running at full capacity, it is surprising how the office can be reformatted to fit in an additional couple of desks, or the warehouse rejigged to include an additional ten pallets, or the van rerouted to make ten additional drop offs each week. Well, guess what, this additional capacity has an opportunity cost for each day that it's under-utilised. Desks are rented at c£500 pcm in London by Weworks and The Office Group, so yours have a definite value depending on your location and the quality of the office and services you are including.

Pursuing this strategy can often seem like a pointless diversion to businesses, but through it, Funding Nav often finds £25k of additional income per annum. This can subsidise an extra staff member or correlate to an additional £250k of added equity value if your business sells on ten times earnings.

There are websites you can use to advertise your capacity, such as sharemyoffice.com, and this is an area where Funding Nav is planning to launch a specific offering, so keep an eye on the website.

There are also a couple of Australian-based trading exchanges. These enable you to trade your surplus capacity, which might have little or no value to you (for example, hotel rooms in winter), with other members who could offer you their own surplus capacity to your benefit. Think of the possibilities with, say, printing or marketing services. Check out Bartercard and BBX if this is of interest.

Partner or incubate with a large company

For many big businesses, their most effective R&D is in fact M&A (mergers and acquisitions). It happens across all industries but especially in the fast-moving world of tech. However, examples include Coca Cola's purchase of Innocent Smoothies, McDonald's purchase of Pret and Google's purchase of *DocVerse*, which allowed Google to accelerate the adoption of its Google Docs product. In fact, Google has bought a company every two weeks over the last year, and that may well represent the best value exit that the acquired company founders will achieve, since they will get some leverage against the value they will bring to the behemoth. Same with Facebook and Amazon etc.

In a similar way that private equity likes to court businesses in advance of acquisition, ditto large potential trade acquirers. They may offer you free space at their offices, free advice and, most valuable of all, a scaled-up contract that will enable you to create early economies of scale and therefore profit. Google, of course, operate their Campus Incubator in London as well as Madrid, Sao Paolo, Seoul, Tel Aviv and Warsaw as a way to engage with start-ups on an exclusive basis.

John Lewis, the British department store chain favoured by Middle England, is an unlikely source of the latest technology breakthrough. But the retailer is one of an increasingly diverse range of UK companies to invest in home-grown start-ups. They hope that by working with disruptive technologies from an early stage, they will not lose business to them later – or have to buy them out at high valuations. Technology and finance groups, such as Microsoft and Barclays, have been running start-up accelerators for years. They are now being joined by a more unusual cast of peers, including retailers Topshop and Asos, betting group William Hill, and even windscreen repair group Autoglass.

Funding Nav offers specialist matching services in this area, and a really effective service at creating engagement between big businesses and smaller businesses to their mutual advantage.

ICOs

Initial Coin Offerings are unquestionably the bright new shiny thing in the fund raiser's armoury. I am, however, somewhat nervous about including this phenomena in something as permanent as a book because, by the time you read this, the whole thing might have blown over. Or maybe it will have rendered all other fundraising virtually redundant. The explosive recent growth in the value of Bitcoin has heightened investors' (and naysayers') interest in cryptocurrencies over the course of 2017 for sure.

Cryptocurrencies are essentially the same as money, but without the backing of a country to stand behind them. I know many don't agree and point to the high level of failure and fraud but, to be fair, there are numerous examples of currencies that were destroyed by inflation despite having the backing of a nation. There are also examples of value being destroyed overnight by the banning of certain cash denominations, such as high value Indian rupee bank notes and, of course, the introduction of the Euro. This left billions of Lire and Drachma valueless, as their owners were unable to go to the bank to swap them for fear of opening a serious can of money laundering worms.

Money laundering is a major issue with cryptocurrencies according to its critics, but ironically, because it operates on Blockchain technology (which means that every transaction is recorded and indelible), it should theoretically be more difficult to hide dodgy crypto transactions than it is cash ones. There were hundreds of ICOs in 2017 where investors swapped fiat (nation-based) currency for crypto currency. As Bitcoin, the most popular, accelerates in value beyond most investors' reach, they have sought newer tokens that are connected to businesses and are sold at a discount in an Initial Coin Offering. Unlike in a sale of shares, the investor owns no part of the equity of the business, but instead tokens that can be traded on the company's platform. They buy these either because they want to use them in the future as a buyer of the company's services, or because they hope or expect that the tokens will increase in value and that they will be able to sell them at a profit to a secondary investor. It's a bit like investing in the game of Monopoly – not by buying shares in its makers Waddington's, but instead by buying Monopoly currency which then becomes the only way to play the game.

So, how can you use this mechanism to raise money for your business?

Well, first, all the successful ICOs I've seen have used Blockchain at their core and not as an add-on. Therefore, you need to have a Blockchain-based tokenised system of exchange deep within your business model. Then, you need to produce a finite amount of tokens and sell some of them as a way of raising money for your venture. The advantages to the entrepreneur are obvious: there is currently little regulation in this area and you can raise as much money as you like without creating either a debt or equity liability.

The ICO process goes beyond what I've written above, somewhat similar to crowdfunding.

At the time of writing, Funding Nav has yet to facilitate an ICO, but I was recently very close to Cashaa, a start-up that raised $10m in a month by selling Etherium-based CAS tokens in November and December 2017. Their business model is to facilitate the ability of the world's unbanked, especially in the Third World, to transfer value, rather like a Western Union but without the enormous costs and infrastructure. We were also involved in raising funds for an internet marketing business that valued itself at just £2m but, following the production of a white paper, decided that its value had increased to £10m literally in a month pre-ICO.

An example of the issues of lack of regulation and the enormous hunger for tokens is UET, which has raised $215k to date, according to their website. Not that impressive when compared to Cashaa or some of the most successful ICOs of the last year that have raised sums in excess of $100m. However, it is actually quite impressive when you consider that, if any of the investors had bothered to read the white paper that accompanied the raise, they might have noticed that the sponsors were quite clear in stating that UET actually stood for Useless Etherium Token and that its purpose was this message: 'You're going to give some random person on the internet money, and they're going to take it and go buy stuff with it. Probably electronics, to be honest. Maybe even a big-screen television. Seriously, don't buy these tokens.'

For more, go to the hilariously honest https://uetoken.com/.

I know I gave Bernie Madoff as a glowing example of a marketing genius in an earlier chapter, but he only raised $60bn in a lifetime of fraud and deception, and wound up in prison for the rest of his life as a result. Bitcoin founder Satoshi Nakamoto, on the other hand, is now worth a reputed $20bn and rising, and, not only is he not in prison, but no one knows who he is, where he is or whether he really exists at all. Locking him up would be a bit like locking up air. Plus, of course, there's the fact that, despite having created something that appears quite Ponzi-like in that Bitcoin is an investment that has no real investment value – the only true value is in selling to someone who believes that the non-existent value actually does exist – in reality, he hasn't done anything illegal. The reason for that is that Bitcoin investors, like UET investors, should know what they are in for.

So, I know that by writing this book I set myself up as an expert in all these areas, but to answer the question of whether you should raise funding via an ICO, currently I would say, only if you're quick. However, this is subject to change as this market is moving so rapidly.

If you're considering this, then please email me at stephen.sacks@ fundingnav.com so that we can discuss what's happened in the meantime and whether it still looks workable. I'm pretty sure we'll be involved in some fund raising of this nature in 2018, so I look forward to sharing that experience with you, if relevant.

11

Raising Equity

SEIS & EIS

These tax incentives that the UK HMRC makes available to UK income tax payers are enormously important in underpinning the UK market for unlisted equities.

The Seed Enterprise Investment Scheme, and its slightly less beneficial and more grown-up cousin *The Enterprise Investment Scheme*, are the government's tax incentive to UK income tax payers to try to level the playing field between the relatively high risks of investing in the shares of unlisted small companies, relative to the much safer and more liquid investment of investing in listed equities.

They both operate with a similar mechanism, offering income-tax-paying investors in qualifying unlisted companies a series of tax benefits that effectively somewhat underwrite and de-risk their investment.

What are the benefits and stipulations of SEIS for investors?

➤ Investors can receive initial income tax relief of 50% on investments up to £100k per tax year in qualifying shares issued on or after 6 April.

➤ A CGT exemption will be offered in respect of gains realised on the disposal of assets that are reinvested through SEIS in the same year.

> The individual investor can be a director of the company, but not an employee.

> An individual's stake in the company can be no more than 30%.

> SEIS tax relief applies only to recently incorporated companies.

> The company must have 25 employees or fewer, and gross assets of up to £200k.

What are the benefits and stipulations of EIS for investors?

1. Income Tax Relief

There is no minimum investment through EIS in any one company in any one tax year. Tax relief of 30% can be claimed on investments (up to £1m in one tax year), giving a maximum tax reduction in any one year of £300k, provided you have sufficient income tax liability to cover it.

EIS allowances are allocated individually. Therefore, a married couple could invest up to £2m each tax year and be eligible for income tax relief. The shares must be held for at least three years from the date of issue or the tax relief will be withdrawn.

People connected with the company are not eligible for income tax relief on their shares.

2. Capital Gains Tax Exemption (CGT)

Any gain is CGT free if the shares are held for at least three years and the income tax relief was claimed on them. Shares can be held for much longer and therefore potentially enable the investor to accrue their CGT exemption over a long period of time, which can be a great attraction.

3. Loss Relief

If shares are disposed of at a loss, the investor can elect that the amount of the loss, less income tax relief given, can be set against income for the year in which they were disposed of, or income for the previous year, instead of being set off against any capital gains.

4. Capital Gains Tax Deferral Relief

Payment of CGT can be deferred when the gain is invested in shares of an EIS qualifying company. The gain can be made from the disposal of any kind of asset but the investment must be made one year before or three years after the gain arose – connection to the company doesn't matter. Unconnected investors are eligible for relief from both income tax and CGT.

As a company owner, you need to write to HMRC seeking clearance to offer your shares under either of these schemes. Generally speaking, the process takes a few weeks but is relatively straightforward.

Crowdfunding

So, hopefully, you now have clearance from HMRC for one of the above two schemes for your company's shares, as that will help potential investors to offset part of their investment against their overall income tax liability. Crowdfunding offers you an excellent route to raising the capital you need to realise your plans.

The reasons for this are multifold:

➤ The crowd will help you to sense-check your idea before you spend too much time or money on it. The process of raising in this way is symbiotic with your general marketing efforts, as you need to sell the service or product idea and then the shares themselves.

➤ The marketing of the shares will raise your company's profile and ultimately create a crowd of, hopefully, bought-in, shareholding advocates who will, especially in B2Cs, act as your extended salesforce.

➤ You will normally be able to achieve a higher valuation with a crowd of shareholders than you will with a single financial investor. Smaller investors generally do very little due diligence, and are often content to follow a lead investor and get some great rewards (often discounts in the future) from the company.

Raising funds in this way will, realistically, take three to four months and will, frankly, be an enormous diversion of resources for the business away from the general day-to-day management. Often it can be a good idea to bring in a facilitator like Funding Nav to help manage the process.

This process starts with the selection of a platform, and there are numerous options. The two biggest are Crowdcube, with almost half a million people on their data base, and Seedrs, who do slightly more deals but at lower average valuations at the time of writing.

We have a full list of options available in the online resources at www.fundingnav.com. Typically, expect to pay between 5% and 7% of funds raised to the platform you choose on completion of a successful raise.

Having decided on how to manage the process and which platform to use, you will need to create your funding website which basically has three components.

The three components for your funding website:

1. Your pitch plan.

2. Your pitch numbers.

3. Probably most importantly, your pitch film.

You should visit all the sites and see what's working and what's not currently working as a guide to how to proceed.

You then need to create a list of all your potential backers because it will be up to you to build this initial momentum. This takes a lot of balls and effort as you get on the phone and start pitching. Most successful raises have 30% in the bag before they launch, so you'll need to bear that in mind. Without a clear idea of where your lead funding is coming from, then don't waste your time trying to crowdfund as the chances of success are very, very remote indeed.

In deciding how much you need to raise, bear in mind that, with most platforms, the rules are that if you don't achieve your target, then generally you get nothing. You do, however, have the opportunity to overfund, and nothing sells better than 'oversubscribed' as we saw from the example of

The Shed. You will need to come up with a valuation and a rationale, as it's more an art than a science, plus a series of rewards to entice potential shareholders.

All this will take a few weeks. Then the platform will do some checks before you go live.

Initially, your clock will tick up because of the lead investors you've managed to recruit yourself, which will give the impression of momentum. Then it's down to you and your team to start issuing updates online, on the phone and face-to-face to your list of contacts and potential investors. Hopefully, at some point, the crowd will follow you, but in my experience they have a herd mentality so tend to follow success. This is a good reason to keep your initial ask on the low-ish side, because it's easier to build momentum when you are already overfunded. Plus, there are some investment businesses that will look at you at that point. Having said that, you also need to ensure that the initial ask makes your plan doable – if that's all you get and it's not enough then you're going to look pretty stupid.

So, you really need to have *two plans*. The first and cheapest to deliver is the one you wheel out to try to get funded initially. The second stretch plan only gets wheeled out as you get close to reaching your initial goal. This second one has all the bells and whistles and will hopefully get you to where you need to be much more quickly.

Obviously both these plans should be at the same valuation.

For the *second stage plan*, you can change the length of time that you are live on the platform, making it shorter or longer (within reason), and you can reduce your valuation during the raise, which would obviously be retrospective to all the initial shareholders. However, this, of course, is really the last thing you want to be doing as it will throw your credibility into doubt. Much better to get more aggressive on the rewards and be more active on the phones before you even consider doing that.

Once you have (hopefully) reached your funding goal and the raise closes, the platform will do a load of due diligence and spend a frustrating few weeks filling in forms before transferring the funds. One of the failings of most platforms is that you can't touch the money, not even the cash that came through your own network as lead investment, until it has all been through the due diligence process. For businesses that are very short of cash, you can imagine just how frustrating and dangerous this last part of the process is.

An example of how valuation can be boosted in this kind of fund raising is a tailoring business that one of our consultants helped recently. The business was less than two years old in its current form, was turning over a couple of million pounds per year, and losing several hundred thousand pounds. By using a cleverly structured list of investor rewards, they set out to raise £500k at a £10m valuation. Honestly, even I thought that they were being hugely optimistic! However, not only did they raise the £500k but in addition they were overfunded by an additional 80%, so walked away having sold 9% of the business for £900k. Then, within a year, they hit up the same investors and sold an additional £400k of shares at the same valuation. Evidently the investors were motivated by factors other than absolute return, such as EIS, discount rewards and a sense of connection to the brand.

The issue will be for businesses such as these that any downturn in business might see them look to tap up investors again, and they will struggle with valuation.

Angel Networks

One of the places that you should be hitting up in advance of your crowdfunding raise is angel networks. These are a more sophisticated version of the crowdfunding platforms, with hundreds rather than hundreds of thousands of members. The lowest investment on crowdfunding platforms is just £10 and the average is about £2k, but angels start at about £25k and upwards.

Typically, angels will want some kind of representation on your board. This can be a good thing as, hopefully, they will have a load of relevant experience that they can bring to bear. It also means you will need to be really sure that this is a person you can work with – not only in good times, but in bad times too!

If you visit the members section of The UK Business Angels Association, you will find a pretty comprehensive list. However, they are normally overwhelmed with applications, so it's often best to work with an intermediary like Funding Nav to help you form your strategy and make the initial approaches where there are ongoing relationships.

Private Equity and Venture Capital

Often clients confuse these two. Whilst both invest in unlisted growing businesses, the major difference is in their risk profile. Private Equity businesses often build relationships with potential investees over months or years, and invest at scale-up rather than seed stage. Sometimes they will only make one or two investments in a year, and generally these are much larger than VCs.

Venture Capitalists have a much more adventurous approach, as their label suggests. They often invest earlier and with more risk.

Each investment normally has to have the potential to repay the whole fund because their hit rate is so abysmal. So, let's say for example that they have a fund of £50m and they make 50 investments of £1m each. Then each investment needs to have the potential of growing 50-fold, which obviously rules out most companies as a possible investment to them. Typically, out of ten investments they may successfully exit one, and be left with nine in various states between bust and zombie.

If you accept investment from either PE or VC, then you will definitely have them or their representative on your board. You will also need to watch out for ratchets in your agreement with them that will reduce your shareholding should things not go according to the very ambitious plan you would have had to agree to in order to solicit their interest in the first place.

Generally, these businesses dislike working with intermediaries such as Funding Nav, so you will be much better approaching them yourself but you will need support in the background creating a hit list of named leads and creating and refining an investable plan. The problem is that they receive literally hundreds of plans every week, of which they reject the vast majority, so how do you make your proposal stand out? The best chance you have is to make an unsolicited personal approach to one of the main decision-makers. Fortunately, they tend to be reasonably gregarious by nature, so going to the same events as they do and making yourself known to them is a good idea. Good organisations that facilitate these kinds of events include Tablecrowd, The Business Funding Show and the UKBAA. So subscribe to their websites and see what turns up. Funding Nav retains highly specific data on all of the main decision makers and we are happy to help. As with all business contacts, ensure that you follow up through LinkedIn immediately after any meeting, and then check out your new contact's primary contacts to further embed yourself into their world.

Tier 1 Entrepreneur Visa

As a committed Brexit remainer, I find it hard to find much positivity in the UK's decision to Brexit in a world where, increasingly, issues need to be dealt with on a cross-border and global basis. But the likely expansion of the T1 Visa system is a definite exception as it offers a great business advantage. In common with most other countries, potential immigrants to the UK can effectively buy themselves a UK passport for £200k under this system. Currently the system exists for all outside the EU, but post Brexit that will probably include EU citizens too.

Essentially, a qualified investor can receive an initial right to remain in the EU if they invest a minimum of £200k in a UK business. This may ultimately be extended to full citizenship in due course. They need to join the board and work in the business and the business needs to employ two additional (currently EU) workers as a result of their investment.

Most applicants in our experience are currently Chinese graduates who decide that they want to stay and make a life for themselves in the UK after university. Their parents, hopefully, have relevant connections in your business sector back in China. If this is the case, then it's a definite win win, as you get an additional £200k in your bank account, as well as a motivated and connected Chinese-speaking board member to expose and grow your business in the fastest-growing large economy in the world.

This, however, is not an easy or cheap process to undertake. Predictably, there are often several levels of introducing agent in China, plus a lot of Home Office paperwork to complete. The costs can easily run to 15% of the total investment received. In addition, the Home Office needs to be convinced that the whole deal is kosher, and you and the applicant need to be happy about the prospect of working together over the next five years as a minimum.

Post Brexit, it's likely that the volume will increase and shift away from China towards Europe. But currently there's no limit on the amount of Tier 1s that you can employ within your business so, theoretically, it could become a worldwide, self-funded roll-out in itself. So far, the maximum that Funding Nav and its partners have placed in a single business is three Tier 1 investors, each investing £200k.

Unlike many developing country schemes, however, the UK scheme specifically excludes any business related to property, whether investment, rental or management, so if that is your business then this isn't for you. Nevertheless, there is a wall of Chinese money seeking property investment schemes in the UK, so engaging with facilitators such as Etouce, who operate various match-making fairs during the year in Beijing and Shanghai that are heavily property orientated, is a definite way forward.

Funding Nav travels to overseas markets several times per year and engages with immigration agents in the UK in order to help facilitate the matching of businesses with potential investors.

If you feel that a Tier 1 applicant/investor could work well within your business, then please contact me to discuss at stephen.sacks@fundingnav. com.

12

Debt

Once upon a time, this subject was simple: you went to the bank manager whose bank held your account and with whom you'd had a lifelong relationship, and asked for either a term loan or an overdraft facility. Nowadays, you probably have no idea who your account manager actually is, your local branch has long ago become a branch of Pizza Express, and your calls are answered initially by an infuriating robot who can't understand your regional accent, so passes you on to Rashmi in Bangalore – who can't either. Even if you are lucky enough to track down your account manager, what you will find is someone with boundless enthusiasm to sell you insurance and other financial products, who says that the bank really wants to lend you the money but that he needs to submit a report into the credit committee.

Now, this bit is really interesting because banks take totally the opposite view to equity investors at this point. If you ever watch *Dragons' Den*, you will note that often decisions are made to back the man rather than the plan, since plans are redundant the moment they are produced. However, the investee is who the investor will be relying on to sort all the issues out in the long term. Banks, on the other hand, have created this hierarchy of the credit committee that you'll never meet, which takes your personality totally out of their decision. It also allows them to play good cop, bad cop with you because, when the ever-smiling manager comes back after a few weeks to tell you that your application has been declined, he can push the blame onto the credit committee and not screw up his chance of selling you an insurance product that you didn't want in the first place; a bit like PPI back in the day!

Actually, despite rumours to the contrary, the main banks are in fact lending, but generally not in the SME market directly. Oddly, they are lending to the secondary lending market, which then creates more esoteric, exotic and expensive products that are made generally available to you as an SME owner. This means that they have managed to create their own competition, who lend to the SME sector at eye-wateringly high rates, whilst they are at the same time being flooded with cheap money from the Bank of England. God knows why they have chosen to do this. However, regardless, the situation today is that there is money out there but it's quite expensive and highly structured, and is likely to come from one of over 300 (yes, over 300!) alternative lenders. These lenders are getting it generally from the banks, who won't give you a second look directly.

On the whole, unless you have a lot of fixed assets in the business or are massively profitable, all lending will need to be personally guaranteed, and it will be transactional so that the lender can keep tabs on it. Basically, it's asset-based lending which is generally around debtors, stock or fixed assets.

If you'd like a list of the lenders in the market and what they do, then we try to keep an up-to-date data base at www.fundingnav.com.

Types of Debt

These are the main products available, with a short description of each:

» **Overdraft:** ability to have a negative balance in your current account. This is repayable on demand, so be careful!

» **Fixed Term Loan:** an amount of money loaned for a given period (say three years), normally repayable in equal monthly instalments but not necessarily.

» **Factoring:** ability to borrow against your outstanding allowable debtor balances, where the bank effectively buys the debt and manages the collection either with or without debtor insurance.

» **Confidential Invoice Discounting:** as above but where you manage your own debt collection, again either with or without debtor insurance.

» **Revolving Stock Finance:** funding goods that you order, generally where you have a credit-worthy final customer and an invoice discounting facility.

» **Fixed Asset Finance:** lease or HP on fixed assets such as cars or identifiable equipment.

» **Commercial Mortgage:** same as your domestic mortgage but secured on the business's property.

» **Merchant Finance:** forward selling your credit card receipts.

Please email me at stephen.sacks@fundingnav.com to discuss your business's loan requirements, as we have some really great deals and can raise debt funding very quickly (often within a week from our lending panel).

It's generally not a good idea to approach lenders yourself, as undertaking repetitive credit checking will have an ongoing and adverse impact on your credit rating, both from a business and a personal perspective.

PART 3

How to Play

An Introduction to How to Play

This section comprises a week-by-week guide to help you transform your business. Don't read it all at once and try to make multiple changes as it won't work. Read a new section every weekend and think about how it relates to you, your situation and your business. Then come up with a plan as to how you will use that section to your benefit. Most importantly, **TAKE ACTION!** Use the space provided to make notes on steps you could implement.

Ideas on their own are worthless without action.

Use the online tools where applicable too, and don't worry about coming back and revisiting an earlier section later. Action that you take in another section may change your thinking or create an opportunity that wasn't obvious earlier. Not all sections will relate to all businesses at all times.

Hopefully, over each weekend, you will come up with your own weekly plan concentrating on a different part of the business, and start actioning it each week. Gradually, changes will increase and multiply so that, over time, the direction will be set, and the fortunes of you and your enterprise will grow to create the business you dreamt of at the outset.

Week 1 - It's all about you

How do you feel on Sunday evenings?

Honestly, how do you *really* feel?

Can you remember how you used to feel on Sunday evenings when you originally started your business?

Inevitably, over time, we change. Businesses and industries change too and often these changes are misaligned. This can ultimately lead to a miserable existence as you find yourself working in a business or industry that has grown apart from you, or that you have grown apart from.

Money can also have a big impact on our motivation. Do you still need the money in the way that you did? Are you more risk averse than you were?

All these factors and many others can create a yawning gap between us and our business, which can lead to personal anxiety, stress – even depression – and a business that will inevitably underperform.

If you were in a regular job, you might well go and find a new one that suited you better, but it's different when you run your own business.

Your choices are basically to change the direction of the business to one you feel happier with, to sell or close the business down, or to employ new management, which will free you up to do something you'd rather put your mind to.

If things are OK, or OK-ish, it's very difficult to consider issues like these yourself as you lack objectivity. And it's probably not wise to discuss them with staff unless there is someone on the team with whom you have a very high level of trust. Family or friends are better, although they will generally tell you what they think you want to hear.

Ideally this is a discussion to have with your peers – people who are or who have been in a similar situation to you and have their own experiences to share. Joining a mastermind or intimate networking group such as *The Association of Chief Executives, Vistage* or *The Supper Club* can be a helpful step. Once you build trust with your peers, you will value their input and they yours.

Alternatively, hire a business coach or mentor. Try to avoid the corporate guys who've bought a coaching franchise as they will have little ability to empathise or relate to you and your situation. Instead, look for people or organisations that not only have interesting and disruptive IP, but also have coaches who have been where you are now and can help you set your goals and achieve them. I personally coach no more than four or five clients at a time, as it's intensive work and therefore I'm normally totally committed. I do, however, know a number of really good coaches and mentors who get great results, so drop me a line at stephen.sacks@fundingnav.com and I'll steer you in the right direction.

Remember, ultimately the business is here to serve its shareholders and, in the case of SMEs where the owner is also the leader, it's not really about the money but about the satisfaction in creating and living your life's work.

Action

Take time out and speak to people you trust and respect about your own dreams and aspirations.

Be honest with yourself! Make notes of your thoughts about your business, both positive and negative. These can give you clarity and help you to evaluate your feelings and begin to see where change needs to happen.

Create an action plan. There's nothing like a concrete set of steps that you can begin to implement, to inspire you and regenerate your business passion.

Make changes to the business over time that will realign it with your original hopes and dreams.

Fall back in love with what you do. Dig deep to rediscover the original 'why' behind your idea.

Notes:

Week 2 - Are you up to it?

Assuming that the business is still for you or that you've taken advice and started to make some changes to it to better suit yourself, the question remains as to whether you are the right person to run it.

Would you employ yourself now?

Again, as with the questions posed in the previous section, it's not a question you can realistically answer yourself, is it?

Whilst it may be illegal to discriminate on most bases when thinking about employment questions relating to others, it certainly isn't when thinking about your own suitability to run the business.

Increasingly, many industries are youth dominated and one thing for sure is that none of us is getting any younger. Are you finding it more and more difficult to relate to your customers as they employ people who are substantially younger than you are to deal with your business? Frankly, that's what happened to me in the last fashion brand that I ran. I had no problems doing the actual work but I was missing the point rather, I'm afraid to say. Success in business isn't all about travelling to meetings, doing deals and then retiring back to the hotel room to get up-to-date on email, which is what I was doing. No, success in my game was all about doing the deal, air kissing, partying with a load of twenty-somethings, getting out of your head and crawling into bed at about 5am having posted a load of pictures on social media. That's the way to build real rapport and get real success in fashion nowadays. Frankly, at 50, I couldn't be arsed and, to be honest, why would the kids be interested in me anyway? I was old enough to be their dad, wasn't Karl Lagerfeld and had no aspiration to be.

So, I bit the bullet and exited, and it was a good decision!

Are you influential in your industry?

Could you become more influential?

Indeed, could you become a key person of influence in your

industry? That's part of the reason that made me want to write this book.

Perhaps removing yourself from the day-to-day minutiae of your business to build your own standing in the industry through speaking and writing might be of more benefit to both yourself and your business today.

The media and the internet have conspired to create a world where the power and the wealth are becoming increasingly concentrated in the hands of fewer and more influential leaders. The best opportunities are often shared in a small circle of influence initially, before the rejected scraps are shared amongst the rest of the industry.

Retraining yourself to speak better and write better, to take advantage of the numerous opportunities there are to blog, write and speak, and to use those opportunities as stepping stones that build both your own influence and inevitably your company's influence, are probably a better use of your time now than continuing to do what you have always done and getting the results you have always got.

Action

Re-invent yourself within your business. As in the previous exercise, consult with others you trust and ask them to be honest about what they perceive as your strengths and weaknesses. Make a list, then begin to focus on what you do well and how you could invest those talents and abilities more creatively into your enterprise.

Focus on new skills that could be of benefit to you and to the business. Is there anything lacking? What else could you bring to it that would have a positive impact and potentially stimulate growth?

Think of some top influencers either in your own industry, or in other areas. What are they doing right? How are they attracting a following? The internet gives people access to an audience on a global scale. If you'd like to position yourself as an influencer, what steps could you take to make your presence felt on a much wider platform?

Commit to addressing your skills gap. It's never too late to acquire fresh expertise. This could be just the time to look into some new learning or training.

Think about joining an organisation like The Public Speaking Association to learn to speak better. Learn to write better too so that you can express yourself with greater clarity.

Notes:

Week 3 - Is it still the right thing?

In the previous section, I asked whether you would employ yourself today. Perhaps a more fundamental question would be, would you create the business you currently head if you were starting up today?

Think about it. Is your business in a growth or a dying industry?

Is the location still relevant or is it now a hindrance?

Are there changes a new owner would make that you haven't?

As with some of the questions posed in earlier sections, you will probably not be equipped to answer this last one. So it might be a useful exercise to again invite your peers into your business to experience a day in your life, and for you to reciprocate with theirs. There's great potential here for you to be able to offer each other useful feedback. If you took my advice and joined a mastermind group, then this could be a fascinating opportunity for you to swap experiences.

Looking afresh at your business and asking yourself some seriously searching questions is tough but, ultimately, will be of great benefit to you. It will help you to:

» Reconnect with the venture to go on to bigger and better things.

» Make changes to the direction of the venture so that it can go on to bigger and better things.

» Make changes to your own direction so that you can go on to achieve bigger and better things.

Not forcing yourself to face up to these matters may feel more comfortable but will most likely result in time spent just going through the motions (rearranging the deckchairs). However, the unstated issues gnawing away at you from the inside are potentially a disaster down the tracks when, in its own brutal way, the market answers the question you've been avoiding.

Something else to consider is whether the business is realistically (or potentially) able to pay you the income you require in order to fulfill ambitions in other parts of your life. If it isn't, then you should seriously consider making improvements aimed at either growing its core cash-generating ability, or else adding further arms that will quickly help you to grow its success.

Alternatively, is now the time to sell? Realistically, who would buy a business like yours today? Would you?

Action

Take a realistic look at your and your business's performance over the last few years.

Are you making progress?

Is it getting easier?

Do you still find solutions in the face of day-to-day running problems?

Can you see where changes could be made to stimulate growth?

If the answer to these questions is no, then you have a potential issue that you need to realistically address. This is where having a coach or mentor really pays dividends.

Notes:

Week 4 - Have you got the right help?

Reviewing staffing is difficult as there is so much invested in the relationships in an SME business. Over time, people are employed to fill roles which themselves change and, of course, people change too. Then there are changes in the industry and technology to consider, so the chances of a business's staff being the best at any point, even if they were at the outset, is remote.

Ongoing reviews that are at least annual are an absolute necessity. But these really need to be deeply considered from a zero position, so that it becomes less about examining the incremental changes over the time since the last review, and more about re-looking at the whole enterprise, and the relationship and relevance that the role in question has moving forward.

It is likely that this process will cause conflict, as the main objective of the staff member will be to drive their value up relative to the overall value of the organisation, whereas the business goal must always be to push back so that the organisation becomes increasingly less reliant on individuals and is able to drive down costs relative to output.

The threats to the business by way of cheaper overseas or contract workers and artificial intelligence should be viewed as opportunities during this process. Staff under review need to take all these factors into account when proposing changes they would like to their positions post review. Ideally, the culture of the business should be outward looking, progressive, pragmatic and challenging. If this can be achieved then progress can be swifter and happen with less friction.

Action

Set up robust and useful HR systems.

Ask an outside advisor to help you look at the way the business is currently configured compared to how you might configure it if you were starting again.

» Consider whether you have the right people to fill the posts in your ideal organisation. Ask yourself:

» Do they perform consistently?

» Does their ethos fit with the direction you have in mind for the business?

» Do you see them as having the potential to evolve in line with your ideas and ambitions?

» What can they bring to the business in the face of new challenges?

» How flexible might they be in terms of changes within their role?

Set up a pay and benefits structure that actually improves staff performance, and measure that improvement.

Notes:

Week 5 - Train to improve

Ongoing, lifelong training is a key factor of success in today's fast-moving world. It's simply not realistic to complete 20 or so years of education in one's formative years and then follow that with 50 or so years of work before retirement. The tumultuous change that has enveloped us means that we will all experience several careers in our lifetimes and will need ongoing education to deal with that.

Training should start at the top! It needn't be time consuming or onerous but can easily be slotted into even a busy lifestyle with the minimum of fuss. Mentoring and coaching can be delivered face-to-face or remotely. Audio training can be accessed via Amazon's Audible or through podcasts at a zero or negligible cost, and can facilitate the process whilst you're driving, on a train or plane or just walking down the street.

All employees should follow the leader's example and embrace the opportunity to engage in ongoing self-improvement. As Charles Darwin said, *"It isn't the strongest of the species that survives but the one most adaptive to change."* In order for the organisation to both survive and indeed prosper, its members should be constantly evolving and improving. This needs to be inbuilt within the organisation's DNA.

Unquestionably the quickest and safest route to overall improvement is through the improvement of the staff. I know there is sometimes a reluctance on the part of company owners to fund the improvement of its people, as the view is that they could leave, taking their new-found skills with them. Granted this possibility isn't great, but worse would be a workforce of untrained and untalented staff.

Ongoing training isn't just useful in upskilling your people and therefore your organisation. It's also a motivator, as people will be encouraged that you are investing in them and trusting them to employ their new skills in improving the business.

Action

Consider the cost of either having the wrong people doing the wrong things within your business, or of firing the people with the wrong skills and rehiring those with the right skills. Once you've calculated the amount, set aside a proportion for training the staff you already have. This will not only be cheaper but, as you invest in your staff, you will be demonstrating faith in their abilities within their various roles. This should boost productivity and help morale generally within the workplace.

Training need not be overly specific but could also focus on life skills, such as neuro-linguistic programming, which would have a massively positive impact on the organisation as well as its members.

What skills do you feel are currently lacking among your workforce? Explore different avenues of training available and see what it's possible to employ to fill this gap.

Notes:

Week 6 - Motivate your people

Sometimes it's easy to think of all of the resources at your disposal equally, forgetting that people are a very human resource, which means that they can be unpredictable. Some small business owners have never been employees before and, given the normal lack of an HR department, they can struggle with management issues. The key is to create a culture or allow one to exist that people find motivating. Given that you probably spend more time with the team than you do with your family, they are likely to know you quite well so you need to be authentic.

Unless people management is a core skill, I would strongly suggest stepping back from management as soon as the business is able to support a structure. This is because otherwise leaders can become mired in inward-looking management issues that can easily distract them from the main task of directing all the other resources in pursuit of the outward company goals.

People are motivated positively by gaining money, recognition, ownership and satisfaction, and negatively by losing these. And what is almost universally demotivating is a lack of support, a perception of unfairness and politics. However, as organisations grow it is often difficult to avoid these issues, so regular zero-based reviews and exit interviews are important in monitoring the pulse of the organisation. Agitators are toxic and should be rooted out and dealt with before they manage to create widespread issues.

A client of ours who runs a team of medical specialists recently changed their payment structure so that the team were better remunerated for selling ongoing plans rather than individual treatments. And guess what? More profit and happier, higher-earning staff, but only after a lot of initial resistance and inertia relating to the potential change.

Action

Think about what motivates you. Are there any measures you could introduce that might similarly motivate your staff and create a culture in which they feel confident they can thrive?

What about structural changes within the business? What could you facilitate that might result in higher earnings for your team?

Who is with you? Take swift and decisive action to remove anyone on the team who has an agenda that's different to that of the company.

Demonstrate your trust in those who remain by giving them a high level of responsibility, thus creating a better future both for themselves and for the business.

Use profit per employee as a meaningful measure of success that will align yourself and your team, allowing everyone to see that they can make an appreciable difference to their segment of the profit.

Notes:

Week 7 - Improve your location

Location is impactful and for many different reasons.

Obviously, for retail-based businesses that rely on passing trade, location is famously the first, second and third most important factor for their success.

For most other businesses, it's important but not key.

Clearly cost matters to all businesses but being in close vicinity to stakeholders such as staff, suppliers and customers is important too.

As with so many other factors, things shift over time and a regular assessment should take place where location is considered.

Does your business even need a static location or can it in fact operate remotely through serviced offices/meeting spaces and your people's homes. Maybe your company could help another business better amortise its overheads by renting some desks in their offices, as mentioned in part two.

Perhaps consider incubator space as there is tons of it coming online constantly.

Listed on the next few pages are business incubators* and where they're situated that cater for many different stages of business, but typically focus on early to mid-stage companies.

*Business Incubators information has been sourced from https://entrepreneurhandbook. co.uk/incubation-centres/

BUSINESS INCUBATORS

London

Google Campus

Google Campus in London is a well-known hub for tech entrepreneurs. The café is a famous meeting point, the events space is renowned for quality and, of course, the broadband is second to none. They also run a range of educational workshops and events for entrepreneurs. As a meeting point, events space or work base, the campus has a vast amount of benefits for entrepreneurs in London.

Location: London

Level39

Level39 is arguably the most significant incubation space for fintech, retail, cybersecurity and the smart-city technology companies in London, and possibly even the United Kingdom. Based in the heart of Canary Wharf, one of London's financial epicentres, Level39 offers access to innovative amenities and runs a range of fantastic and well-known networking events. Even to rent space or become a member of the incubator, the application process is rigorous. This means that, if lucky, you will be around an elite network of fellow entrepreneurs, investors and business leaders.

Location: London

White Bear Yard

White Bear Yard is one of London's best kept entrepreneurial secrets, housing some of the city's significant start-ups, including Angel List and Tide. It also houses one of the UK's most prolific and respected early-stage investors, Passion Capital. They have office hours, a range of events and always a lot going on. The monthly desk price includes super-fast WiFi, shower rooms, full kitchen, free lunch once a month and much more.

Location: London

IDEALondon

One of the more recently started business incubation centres, IDEALondon is owned and managed by University College London. The centre is not limited purely to students/graduates, but is open to all current, or soon-to-be current, London based early-stage digital technology ventures. There is also a range of investors based at IDEALondon, as well as government schemes such as Capital Enterprise. The centre is a hub for some of London's most innovative companies, and provides all the standard amenities and a great community.

Location: London

London BioScience Innovation Centre (LBIC)

Based in London and managed by the Royal Veterinary College, the London BioScience Innovation Centre (LBIC) was initiated in 2001. The incubator provides life science companies with state of the art lab facilities, office space and much more.

Location: London

London Cleantech Cluster

A clean energy incubator founded in 2012, London Cleantech Cluster specialises in supporting renewable and clean energy businesses and technology development. The cluster brings together many cleantech initiatives in London, and will provide cleantech businesses with access to mentors, office space, and a like-minded community for entrepreneurs building sustainable energy production alternatives.

Location: London

Seedcloud

As an incubator for B2B companies, Seedcloud has been based in London since 2012. They provide a range of support to start-ups, with particular focus on creating a clear roadmap for entrepreneurs, building formidable go-to market strategies and finding suitable seed investors. All the standard facilities are included, such as office space, accountancy support and legal advice from partners.

Location: London

Breed Reply

Founded in 2014, Breed Reply is an incubation programme based in central London and managed by the Reply Group, a consulting, systems integration and digital services company. They provide incubator spaces to start-ups developing digital technologies in the IOT space, and offer direct funding options coupled with office space, networking, events and more.

Location: London

Imperial College White City Incubator

The Imperial College White City Incubator is an incubator programme run by Imperial College, London. It offers incubation facilities for start-ups involved in deeptech, life sciences, engineering and manufacturing. Alongside workspace, it provides a range of virtual office services.

Location: London

Techtopia

An incubator for new start-ups and existing small companies wishing to grow, Techtopia provides serviced office space, investor access and many other amenities to technology-based SMEs. They also boast having a network of successful entrepreneurs who form the basis of their office community.

Location: London

Rain Cloud

Rain Cloud is a specialist accelerator for supporting start-ups who are working to create and build the next generation of civtech start-ups (technology that improves the lives of citizens). The incubator is based in London Victoria and provides access to office space and mentorship.

Location: London

Tech Hub

Tech Hub is a well-known office provider and innovation space across the world, particularly in the UK and Europe. Founded by the editor of Tech Crunch and other co-founders, Tech Hub has become a significant provider of network/events space and much more for tech start-ups.

Location: London (also in Swansea so listed again under WALES)

Innovation Warehouse

Innovation Warehouse are an essential incubator space to include here due to the sheer amount of services they provide. Based in the old fish market in Central London, as well as providing office space, Innovation Warehouse offer access to a sophisticated angel network. They also boast a great event space and have Accelerator Academy, Capital Enterprise and City of London as partners, among others.

Location: London

Central Working

Started by James Layfield, a well-known British entrepreneur, Central Working is a popular entrepreneurial co-working and innovation space in the United Kingdom. CW work on a club model that's focused on building a mix of events and excellent space/environment. They also guarantee a vast experience in the first 30 days, or else you get your money back!

Location: London (also in Manchester so listed again under WIDER ENGLAND)

Impact Hub

Impact Hub, particularly in London, is well known for being an excellent space for freelancers and small businesses/tech start-ups. They run tours at 3pm every Tuesday and 2pm every Friday for anyone looking to check it out in Westminster.

Location: London and International

London Business School Incubator

A total support incubation programme for start-ups run by the London Business School, members can get access to all the university's facilities, including office, professional services, research and academic materials. Start-ups are initiated into the incubator in cohorts of ten, and you will also be given mentoring and further expert support to help progress your business. To be eligible for the London Business School Incubator, you must base yourself in London and be alumni of the university.

Location: London

Wider England

Nest

First built in 2016, the Nest is an incubator run by the University of Portsmouth. It's available to current students and students who have graduated in the last five years. The incubator is for very early-stage businesses with many ideas, supporting entrepreneurs from business idea to business creation. The Nest also provides classes on raising investment, running a business and more.

Location: Portsmouth

Tetricus Incubator

Created in 2000, the Tetricus Incubator is an incubation programme run by the Porton Science Park. It focuses on incubating life science companies and has a sophisticated network in place ideal for any new or growing biotech business to utilise in developing further. The incubator can provide both lab and office space and is already home to a high number of biotech businesses.

Location: Wiltshire

Entrepreneurs For The Future

Entrepreneurs For The Future is an incubator that can provide up to six months of support for new entrepreneurs and start-ups in the Birmingham area. Benefits of the start-up incubator programme include access to experienced entrepreneurs in residence, development of robust action plans for development, and one-to-one sessions with experts on how to grow your business.

Location: Birmingham

Advanced Technology Innovation Centre (ATIC)

The Advanced Technology Innovation Centre (ATIC) provides a business incubator programme based at Loughborough University. The programme offers flexible terms for renting space, café facilities, bike storage, electric car charging, meeting rooms and more. It's aimed at new deeptech businesses and those looking to scale.

Location: Loughborough

The Hive

The Hive is a well-regarded Midlands business incubator run by the Nottingham Trent University, with an 80% survival rate of businesses up to three years after incubation. It provides a range of solutions and services to start-ups, including workspace, meeting rooms, mentoring and more.

The incubator has been one of the premier choices for start-ups and early-stage businesses in the Derbyshire and Nottinghamshire areas since it was founded in 2001.

Location: Nottingham

Evolve Derby

Founded in 2013, Evolve Derby is an incubation programme run by the University of Derby and based in the Derby, Derbyshire, Nottingham and Nottinghamshire areas. The incubator offers a range of services to start-ups including office/workspace, seminars/workshops and mentoring.

The University of Derby's business support and incubation service is there to give you the best possible chance of success, helping you access all the support you need to establish and grow your business, wherever you are located.

Location: Derby

MedTech Incubator

Founded in 2010, the MedTech Incubator specialises in incubating businesses developing digital technologies that could be used by the NHS to improve patient care. The incubator is based in Manchester Science Park and can provide medtech businesses with workspace and networking, plus access to state-of-the-art design and manufacturing facilities.

Location: Manchester

Central Working

Started by James Layfield, a well-known British entrepreneur, Central Working is a popular entrepreneurial co-working and innovation space in the United Kingdom. CW work on a club model that's focused on building a mix of events and excellent space/environment. They also guarantee a vast experience in the first 30 days, or else you get your money back!

Location: Manchester (also in London so listed again in LONDON section)

3M Buckley Innovation Centre (3MBIC)

The 3M Buckley Innovation Centre (3MBIC) is a University of Huddersfield-run business incubator offering support to businesses in the Leeds City area. The incubator boasts fantastic scientific facilities, including laboratory space with all the typical incubator support/amenities. The facility is a purpose-built innovation centre to encourage business growth and collaboration between start-ups/ SMEs and academia.

Location: Huddersfield

Newcastle Bio Incubator

Started by the University of Newcastle in 2016, the Newcastle Bio Incubator is located in the medical school within the university, offering incubator spaces for companies of between two and five people. They're explicitly looking for early-stage companies with some traction in the life science/health arenas, and can provide laboratory and research space alongside usual office facilities.

Location: Newcastle

Cloud Innovation Centre

The Cloud Innovation Centre is a joint initiative from the Cloud Innovation Centre (CIC), Newcastle University Digital Institute and Newcastle City Council. As an incubator, the centre focuses on providing space and support for digital technology businesses, particularly those developing cloud technologies or technology in big data analytics. They are looking for early-stage start-ups and offer access to experts, networks and technology events alongside office space.

Location: Newcastle

MyIncubator

Wenta, the overall company, runs six incubators across the UK. They hold a range of events, training/educational seminars and much more. If you meet specific requirements, you may get three months free.

Location: Bedford, Luton, Potters Bar, Stevenage, Watford and Ware

Wales

Cardiff Medicentre

Built in 1992, the Cardiff Medicentre is situated in East Wales. This business incubator focuses on providing lab and office facilities for health and wellbeing, life science and biotech companies. Aside from specialist medical services and labs, it offers a range of support in the form of funding advice, networking and access to further expertise. The incubator is run as an economic development project by Cardiff and Vale University Health Board in partnership with Cardiff University.

Location: Cardiff, South East Wales

ICE Accelerator

Although described as an accelerator, from the more traditional accelerator definition, the ICE Accelerator is more of an incubator programme by Welsh ICE for the support of early-stage technology businesses. They're especially looking for companies that want to base themselves in Wales but trade beyond Welsh/UK borders. ICE is funded by the Business Wales Growth Programme in conjunction with the European Region Development Fund.

The incubator is designed to support companies in the immediate area but also other businesses from around Wales. They can provide access to direct funding, mentors and more.

Location: Caerphilly, South East Wales

Institute of Life Science Incubator

Based in Swansea, the Institute of Life Science Incubator is a business incubator with the aim of supporting advances in medical science to improve human health by incubating life science companies. The incubator can provide access to lab spaces, experts and working space, with a competitive package for any business.

Location: Swansea

Centre for Nanohealth Incubator

Founded by Swansea University in 2014, the Centre for Nanohealth Incubator provides a range of services and amenities to life science companies developing the latest nanotechnology. These services include access to nanotech experts, legal and accountancy advice, lab space and office space. The centre has been designed as a state-of-the-art nanotechnology facility through the award of a £22m government investment.

Location: Swansea

Tech Hub

Tech Hub is a well-known office provider and innovation space across the world, particularly in the UK and Europe. Founded by the editor of Tech Crunch and other co-founders, Tech Hub has become a significant provider of network/events space and much more for tech start-ups.

Location: Swansea (also in London so listed again in LONDON section)

Scotland

European Marine Science Park

Since 2005, the European Marine Science Park has been dedicated to providing service to early-, mid- and late-stage marine science companies. The incubator is based in a remote area of the highlands and offers fantastic access to untouched nature and ocean environments. It is also open to life science, energy and environmental companies.

The incubation programme offers workspaces, lab space, direct funding from the Park, as well as mentorship coupled with legal and financial support. It also enjoys significant links with academia, research institutions and policy makers in governments, beneficial to any company.

Location: Argyll

Seed Haus

Founded in 2017, Seed Haus is located in eastern Scotland, more specifically Edinburgh. The incubator provides a range of facilities and services including mentorship, seminars, investment advice, network access, start-up events, as well as legal and accountancy support through partners.

The Seed Haus team look for start-ups who are solving significant problems and will benefit from their expertise.

Location: Edinburgh

Northern Ireland

Centre for Secure Information Technologies (CSIT)

Founded in 2008, the Centre for Secure Information Technologies (CSIT) is a start-up and business accelerator for new ventures developing solutions and technologies in the cybersecurity space. The incubator is run by Queen's University of Belfast and is available for cybersecurity start-ups and companies in the Northern Ireland area.

They can offer start-ups a range of support including mentoring, technology/development support, investment training and more.

Location: Belfast

Innovation Factory

The Innovation Factory provides flexible office space alongside business incubation services including mentorship, networking and more. It also has a range of flexible spaces for co-working, shared working and meetings/events, alongside virtual address services. The incubator is suitable for all types of SME.

Location: Belfast

START-UP INCUBATORS

The incubators below are entirely focused on supporting businesses who have yet to start up and entrepreneurs who have just begun their businesses. The programmes typically offer some excellent benefits to new businesses, beyond the usual accelerator perks, including reduced-rate or free office space and, in some cases, grants or small direct investment.

London

Bathtub 2 Boardroom

Established in 2010, Bathtub 2 Boardroom is a not-for-profit company that provides an excellent incubator space and support programme for young entrepreneurs just starting out. Given their objective, their membership/office space rental fees are meagre compared to typical incubators or co-working spaces in London.

Alongside affordable office space, they can provide you with meeting rooms, networking events, funding advice and a fantastic community of fellow entrepreneurs to engage with.

Location: London

Health Foundry

Founded by the Guy's and St Thomas' Charity, since 2016 the Health Foundry has been running as an incubator for start-ups in the health and wellbeing space. They're focused on supporting start-ups that create or apply digital technology in innovative ways to improve the wellbeing and health of people. They also provide demo days for fundraising, network access and legal/financial training and support. If you are a healthtech start-up, this is one of the more obvious incubator choices.

Location: London

UCL BaseKX

Created by University College London (UCL) in 2010, UCL BaseKX is a business incubator that supports new start-ups in the Kings Cross area of London. Aside from office space in central London, you can benefit from expert seminars, mentorship, demo days and help from UCL's innovation and enterprise team in turning your idea into a successful business.

Location: London

City Ventures Launch Lab

First launched in 2013, the City Ventures Launch Lab is an incubation programme for graduates and students of City University London. The centre is based in the middle of tech city, London, and the incubator offers members networking events, training and much more.

Location: London

Open Education Challenge

Started in 2014, Open Education Challenge is an incubator for European EdTech start-ups developing and delivering the next generation of education technologies and related tech. The incubator was initially started in collaboration with the European Commission and endeavours to bring together education practitioners and innovative entrepreneurs to develop innovative edtech. The incubator can provide space, edtech network access and much more.

Location: London

Wider England

Sussex Innovation Croydon

Begun in 2015, Sussex Innovation Croydon is a business incubator programme run by the University of Sussex alongside the area's local enterprise partner, Coast to Coast Capital. The incubator provides members/start-ups with office space, workspace, network access and investment readiness training, alongside other financing advice. It's a community for entrepreneurs building early-stage ventures.

Location: Croydon

Portsmouth Technopole

Portsmouth Technopole, established in 2009, is an epicentre for new businesses in the Solent area. The incubator is run by Portsmouth University and is geared towards start-ups developing digital technology projects with specifics in fields including energy and environment.

The incubator offers first-rate support to SMEs, including flexible workspace, virtual office services, incubator offices, conference rooms and more.

Location: Portsmouth

Oxford Start-Up Incubator

Established in 2011, the Oxford Start-Up Incubator is managed by Oxford University Innovation. The incubator focuses on providing support to companies before starting out (typically for eight months before incorporation or less) that have come out of Oxford University's eco-system (staff, students and recent graduates).

The incubator can also provide investment funding, expertise and introductions to investors for technology and digital startups.

Location: Oxford

Manchester Incubator Building

Founded in 2005, the Manchester Incubator Building is an incubation programme run by the University of Manchester. They tend to focus on incubating start-ups in the life sciences space, providing a range of services including office and laboratory space, and a variety of other infrastructures useful to deeptech companies, biotech firms, satellite companies carrying out R&D, and even pharma companies looking to develop drugs.

Location: Manchester

Genesis

Founded in 2001, Genesis is a business incubation programme run by the Barnsley Business & Innovation Centre and based in the Leeds. Offering a range of services and support to start-ups, the incubator assists entrepreneurs by providing flexible office space, funding advice, access to angel investors and legal/accountancy support through partners.

The incubator's focus is on business development, aiming to accelerate companies predominantly regarding sales, customers and overall commercialisation.

Location: Cudworth

The Duke of York Young Entrepreneur Centre

The Duke of York Young Entrepreneur Centre is a start-up incubator operated by the University of Huddersfield. The incubator supports staff, recent graduates and current students of the university in starting and growing their own business in Leeds. You can be starting a company, becoming a freelancer or becoming self-employed in some way to qualify for access to the centre. There is also an enterprise team on hand to help you with every aspect of starting or running a business.

Location: Huddersfield

Scotland

CodeBase

CodeBase is one of the UK's largest start-up incubators and focuses on providing support to more than 100 digital technology companies at any one time. At CodeBase, there is a community of diverse technology entrepreneurs, all in the early stages of their venture. You can get access to experts with an expansive range of skills, as well as serious business and development support.

Location: Edinburgh

Bright Red Triangle

Established in 2004 by the Edinburgh Napier University, Bright Red Triangle is an incubation programme. As a start-up incubator, it offers students and graduates of the university who are starting, or who want to start, their own business, access to desk space, advice, to a like-minded entrepreneurial community and more.

Location: Edinburgh

RGU Incubator

From Robert Gordon University and Accelerate Aberdeen, the RGU Incubator is an incubation programme providing students and graduates of the university with access to workspace, mentorship and advice right through from initial idea, to setting up a company, to running a successful company or business.

Location: Aberdeen

Action

Consider the accessibility and location of the ideal home for your business relative to its current location and the cost of upheaval.

What are the benefits of staying where you are?

Would changing location offer any opportunity to expand, if that's your aim?

If it's a consideration, could moving positively or negatively affect your visibility as a company?

Look closely at the way your business functions and consider whether it actually needs a location at all or whether you could operate efficiently without somewhere fixed.

Notes:

Week 8 - Improve your environment

This is a very difficult area to get right as perception is a major factor.

Working from a plush environment impresses some and worries others. It certainly varies by industry but also within industries.

Tidiness is universally important, but spending a ton of cash on a marble fountain in the atrium is probably over the top. You can lose customers by appearing overly ostentatious or overly basic.

Fortunately, it's possible nowadays to appear both stylish and economic through an astute choice of design for the work environment.

Action

Spend time thinking about your business's environment and what would be ideal. Could you create more space? Could you utilise any areas more effectively?

With some ideas in mind, ask office refurb companies to come in and plan what's possible.

Even if you can't afford to action the changes now, stick the plans up in the office and use them as an incentive to motivate the team to meet a specific milestone.

Tidy up! Over time, people fill desk drawers and desk tops, filing cabinets, and every other nook and cranny with crap – including virtual crap on your server. Use a quarterly tidy up as an opportunity to take stock, sometimes literally and sometimes metaphorically.

Encourage your staff to personalise their specific workspace to reflect their own characters. I visited the offices of Amazon subsidiary, Zappos in Las Vegas, and they had created a dynamic environment by giving their people a small budget to customise their particular spaces.

Week 9 - Improve your software

We're back to Moore's Law again. This is massive! The speed of change means that there are huge efficiency savings available to every industry. The cost of not being abreast of these could mean terminal failure as competitors overhaul you.

Sometimes you will need to bite the bullet and accelerate the rate at which you write down or write off existing packages. Or you might develop software yourself to give your business a competitive edge. This could also represent a whole new area of activity and a new profit centre for you.

Bear in mind the R&D reclaim opportunity of undertaking your own software developments that was discussed previously.

Action

Carry out an in-depth market survey of competitors and the technology they employ.

Is there anything obvious that would help you to seriously improve efficiency? When considering your options, remember:

» The cost of software has plummeted.

» Often it can be bought as a service, so paid for in instalments rather than invested in up front.

» So many tasks have been revolutionised over recent years by the acceleration in the performance of software.

» Even typing may be redundant as voice recognition alters the way that we interact with our machines.

» Virtual meeting software that is essentially free, such as Skype and Zoom, can massively increase efficiency as travel becomes far less necessary.

» Artificial intelligence means that many mechanical tasks no longer need to be done by staff.

» AI and VR, if used properly, have the potential to revolutionise sales processes and can already be seen in use by professions such as estate agents, thereby reducing the need to visit properties in person.

Spend time with the senior team in the business doing some blue-sky thinking about issues and how technology can be better employed to resolve them.

Measure your efficiency levels now and imagine how they will improve if Moore's Law continues, provided that you stay abreast of what's happening.

Notes:

Week 10 - Improve your hardware

Deteriorating hardware is like being a frog, boiled alive. You simply don't notice how old hardware failures and slowness eats into your time and to the time of your people. One of the things most likely to throw this into sharp relief is downloading new software. Generally, people make do and patch up until the position becomes untenable. However, given that Moore's Law is making hardware much cheaper and quicker every year, but not people, you really need to be writing off and replacing hardware before you notice how it is negatively impacting your productivity.

When you consider that the opportunity cost of an hour of your time is probably way in excess of £100 and you may spend at least an hour a week waiting on or rebooting your computer (which would probably cost no more than £1,000 to replace), you can start to appreciate the economic argument.

You will probably be able to lease this kit over a three-year period if cash flow is an issue and get your payback in the first 12 weeks.

Action

Think about the efficiency of the equipment you use. Has there been noticeable drop-off in performance?

Nowadays, so many entrepreneurs run their businesses from laptops and mobile phones because of their adaptability and flexibility. We are, all of us, totally reliant on these devices. Understanding that we need to stay ahead of the game and always up-to-date with the latest developments as our demands get greater is vital. So review your current technology. Is anything stopping you from upgrading? If it's a question of finance, spend some time looking into how your business's overall efficiency could be increased with time-saving and better equipment.

It's a good idea to ask your IT supplier to run speed and capacity tests across the network and, where necessary, augment and replace kit.

Double check the business's contingency against a computer meltdown through backups and off-siting. (This is less necessary now that we routinely use the cloud but you'd be surprised what we find with our clients.)

Notes:

Week 11 - Cut your main input costs

This is a big one and pretty key to your business's viability. However, sometimes it's difficult to achieve since there are vested interests in a business retaining the status quo. Regrettably, though, the status quo is illusory and, in reality, businesses are rarely stable but are either contracting or expanding.

Every process, service and product should be regularly put out to tender and the status quo should be tested. Suppliers must be kept under pressure constantly, otherwise they will gradually alter deals in their favour, either through increasing prices or decreasing quality or service. Sometimes it can be a good idea to work together with suppliers or competitors towards a mutually strategic goal, so that there is an additional benefit to you and you can gain greater knowledge or control of the market place.

This can at times lead to consolidation in the market, which can be highly beneficial, by removing costs and increasing volume and profitability.

An external advisor can be very helpful in this area to really challenge the business.

Action

Train staff to negotiate. Their expertise in this area is vital for the economic running of your enterprise.

What are your business's ten largest areas of expenditure? Make a list and analyse these costs. If possible, ask the supplier to break down their costing so that you can properly understand how they arrive at it.

Look at alternative suppliers and processes. Have you considered AI or going overseas? Could you form any strategic alliances with suppliers, customers or competitors?

Try to understand the motivation and costs of your supplier with a view to creating a mutually advantageous arrangement that will drive costs down.

Notes:

Week 12 - Cut your ancillary costs

Whilst the absolute size of ancillary and peripheral costs to the business is likely to be much less than the main input costs, the proportional efficiency to be gained is much larger since the business has far less visibility and control over areas such as foreign exchange, utilities, transport and insurance etc. In aggregate, however, these costs could be at least as much as the main input costs, so again need to be put out for tender on an ongoing basis.

Often suppliers are very switched on to the fact that there is far less price elasticity with ancillary products and services, and will ensure that they earn much larger margins in these areas.

Action

How could you efficiently monitor your ancillary costs?

Why not consider seconding someone, such as a virtual assistant with appropriate expertise, to the business? They could be tasked with carrying out ongoing price comparisons together with invoice analysis to make sure that the business is always paying the best price and buying in the most economical way.

This is definitely an area where calling in a specialist such as Funding Nav can be a distinct advantage. We are constantly combing the market looking at costs and then buying in volume by consolidating a lot of our clients into volume contracts.

Don't underestimate the savings you could make if you tackle and keep on top of this issue. These costs may be termed 'ancillary', but the value of scrutinising them on a regular basis could be significant to your business.

Notes:

Week 13 - Stimulate demand

First, do you know your two key marketing numbers?

» Average cost of customer acquisition.

» Average lifetime customer value.

It's only when you know these numbers that you can accurately plan an effective marketing campaign. Measuring everything as much as possible is vital, since most businesses need to recruit profitably and different strategies will throw different numbers. For example, different acquisition strategies can buy different levels of loyalty and therefore lifetime value.

Secondly, get more out of your existing customers by taking an 80/20 view of your customer base, because it's highly likely that 80% of your profit is coming from your top 20% of customers. Ensure that you concentrate 80% of your resources into customer retention on that top 20%.

Action

Calculate your average customer acquisition cost and average lifetime customer value, and sense-check all customer acquisition activity against these numbers.

Use the Equation Of Business tool on the Funding Nav website as a reference.

Do some research into incentives on offer by individual companies to increase demand within your industry. What could you offer to your loyal customers?

Analyse which are your top 20% of customers and visit them yourself to find out what more you could be doing to build their loyalty and levels of business.

Notes:

Week 14 - Increase prices

This is massive! One of the most common misconceptions in business relates to a lack of elasticity of pricing amongst customers. Most businesses live in fear of losing customers to cheaper competitors. However, price is just one of the parameters guiding your customers' decision-making process.

If your net margin now is 10% and you increase your prices by 10% then, if all things remain as they are, your net profit will much more than double. So you could afford to lose a substantial amount of business before you are worse off – probably in the region of 30%. If possible, trial new pricing selectively and disguise increases by packaging up products and services so that you increase customer benefits at the same time. This will make any price rises less obvious.

Generally, margins corrode over time as various hits to costs are absorbed and not properly reflected in the selling price. Work hard to counter this by raising prices ahead of the curve.

In the unlikely event that there is a threatened mass loss of customers, then it would be best to regroup, get out of the commoditised area you are in by aiming at niches, and try again.

Use dynamic pricing such as almost all fixed supply/variable demand businesses already do, for example airlines and hotels. Don't just use this technique seasonally but also on a daily basis if appropriate, much as bars do with happy hour.

I had a client who rented camper vans whose big claim was that he offered consistent pricing all year round. He told me that this was disruptive to the market. When I first visited him on a freezing March morning, I counted the camper vans in his parking area and, through a process of elimination, calculated that he had rented none that day. When I checked his records, that was pretty much the story throughout the previous winter. He was, however, pretty booked up for the summer and booked for years for the Glastonbury weekend. I pointed out to him that his pricing was like a broken clock that is dead right twice a day, but wrong all the rest of the time. We discussed increasing his prices in the high season and reducing them in the low season.

As it happens, he didn't take the advice as he was so wedded to his flat pricing concept, so we parted ways. Pricing is a very emotive subject, as I've said, and sometimes entrepreneurs are loathe to mess with it, even when it's obviously broken.

Action

Have a good look at your pricing. Can you see where increases can and should be made?

When you do increase your prices, do so intelligently so that you can begin to feel the point at which demand starts to drop off.

Use the Equation Of Business tool on the Funding Nav website as a reference.

Experiment with dynamic pricing to keep your capacity as close to 100% at all times.

Offer good, better, best options to give your customers the choice to trade up if they wish.

Make sure to monitor sales following a price hike, in particular among your top 20% of customers.

Notes:

Week 15 - Cut finance costs

I know we've already covered funding in section 2 quite exhaustively, but I just want to touch on it again, because sometimes the costs can creep up on you and it's worth reviewing on an ongoing basis and keeping in check.

Ultimately, successful and sustainable businesses are funded by the profits and cash flow generated by their trading activities.

Additional funding is often required at various stages of a business's development, but you should be wary of becoming overly reliant on it.

Often a cut in funding will occur naturally as a bonus if you adopt some of the other strategies discussed, such as increasing prices to push up margin and profits. This may have a positive impact on revenue that will most likely reduce any funding required.

Cutting inventory and costs will also cut funding.

External funding is a dead weight of cost and risk. It is positive in that it magnifies growth but if things get tough then it can leverage that too and create a lack of focus on the business fundamentals.

What you should always bear in mind is that external funding brings external responsibility and will lessen your control and increase the workload of reporting.

There are basically two different routes:

» Debt.

» Equity.

Debt is cheaper unless the business fails. In this case it may well need to be repaid preferentially and not die with the company, since it's common for directors to be asked to guarantee.

Equity is cheaper if the company fails but can be massively expensive if it succeeds. Remember the guy that painted a wall for Facebook back in the day? He accepted shares in lieu of payment and wound up a millionaire as a result.

Of course, there are so many variants and hybrids to consider that it's worth spending time looking very closely at this whole area, and certainly not accepting the first deal you're presented with.

Action

Consider every option to cut exposure to external funding. How else can you drive your business forward in monetary terms? Make a list of your thoughts and ideas and keep it somewhere where you will see it on a regular basis. Then it can serve as a prompt to motivate you to keep on top of this aspect of your enterprise.

Re-read section 2 of this book regularly as a basic reference and spend some time exhaustively going through the grant section. Check online, too, to keep up-to-date with funding changes.

Renegotiate funding deals to bring down costs or increase flexibility.

Look into getting paid more quickly whilst at the same time paying suppliers more slowly.

Notes:

Week 16 - Cut taxes

No one likes paying taxes!

However, unfortunately there isn't much option, although this is definitely an area where it might be worth investing in some good advice.

It's every business leader's duty to pay the minimum amount of tax that is legally permissible. Good examples of businesses that do this very obviously are Arcadia, whose major shareholder, Mrs Green, is a tax exile and therefore receives all her dividends free of tax, and Starbucks, which has used transfer pricing strategies to shift profits to low tax jurisdictions. I know it isn't fashionable to say this as it's an affront to public sentiment but, honestly, any CFO who doesn't try their best to legally mitigate their company's exposure to taxes is not doing their job properly. If government don't like it then they should change the rules.

There are also numerous tax breaks available to companies, such as capital allowances for investment in infrastructure, and research and development (R&D) tax credits for risky investment in novel ideas, which have been covered in section 2.

Tax breaks are available, too, to shareholders, such as the Seed Enterprise Investment Scheme and the Enterprise Investment Scheme, both of which make investing in SME businesses less risky and more attractive, again as already covered.

Nowadays, there is little difference between shareholding directors receiving their income by way of salary or dividends, in which case I personally would choose salary because it may be partly reclaimable with R&D and, if it all goes wrong, you can't be asked to repay it.

The other fabulous tax break that the UK HMRC offers is Entrepreneurs' Relief. This relief offers shareholding directors that meet certain conditions a discounted rate of 10% on capital gains made as a result of a company sale, with a lifetime maximum value of £10m.

Action

Talk to your peers to see who can recommend a good advisor.

Talk to several advisors and see who makes most sense.

As with legal advice, regretfully you get what you pay for here which means the best advice that will save you the most in the long term probably won't be cheap in the first instance.

Notes:

Conclusion

Business is a wonderful thing. Your business can be a wonderful thing, however you may feel about it right now.

It doesn't really matter what was in the past as you can't change that, but what you can do is re-imagine your business today, go and get your vision funded and deliver your company and yourself a better and more prosperous future. If you get it right, it will support you, make you wealthy and keep you gainfully employed in a role that you love, which means that you'll hardly notice the effort. However, get it wrong and you could literally make yourself ill and lie awake every night.

The difference between these disparate outcomes is vast and only you can bridge that gap.

Stay honest with yourself above all else and remember that the roles of owner and CEO are not necessarily synonymous.

Just because you own the business, that doesn't automatically mean you are the best person to run it on a day-to-day basis.

You could become chairperson as well as continuing to add value in the role you excel in, and delegate the day-to-day managing director's role to someone else.

Beware the myth of social media. Facebook likes or favourited tweets are not deliverable results in themselves, regardless of what any agency tells you. What is important is your ability to leverage that sentiment into cash.

Always look for value and question everything with a childish naivety. Just because we always did it that way or always bought from a specific vendor, that's not necessarily a reason to continue.

Slash inventory wherever possible as stock can be the silent killer that overtakes your business. More stock equals more finance, less stock turn, higher storage charges and write downs, and will keep your prices lower than they should be. Keep the market keen!

Success is all about behaviour and use of time, so break the rules. Don't be afraid of a messy kitchen; fail quickly and be immune to fear, criticism and worry. Industry rules and norms are bullshit so don't follow them – disrupt them.

Finally, it's impossible to get rich on income alone, so you need to be building equity from an early stage. Nowadays, that generally means developing your own intellectual property in whatever form is relevant to your industry.

There is lots of additional information, including constant updates and worksheets, available to you as a reader of this book at www.fundingnav. com. You should use this as an ongoing and dynamic resource, so hop over to the website as often as you like. I or a member of my team can be reached at stephen.sacks@fundingnav.com if you have any specific questions.

Just remember, action gets results – doing nothing or staying the same will only fetch you the same, or probably even less, than you are getting today. If you really want to re-imagine your business, get it funded and grow it, I can't stress enough the importance of completing all the action points in this book, as well as making full use of the online resources and of our team here at Funding Nav.

Good luck.

Stephen Sacks.

References

Page 27 – BBC News article from http://www.bbc.co.uk/news/business-32824770

Page 34 – Jim Collins – *Good to Great*, first published in 16 October 2001 by William Collins.

Page 42 – *Fortune 500 Firms Publication* - The Fortune 500 is an annual list compiled and published by Fortune magazine.

Page 76 – Youtube url of *The Shed* at Dulwhich https://www.theshedatdulwich.com/ (follow the link at the bottom for facebook, and then watch the video from Vice.

Page 96 – Grants section has been sourced from https://entrepreneurhandbook.co.uk/grants-loans/ and was accurate at the time of print.

Page 191 – Business Incubators information has been sourced from https://entrepreneurhandbook. co.uk/incubation-centres/

About Me

I have literally had a lifetime of experience in business (or at least 35 years) and I've always worked for myself. This is largely because I was a total failure at school, leaving with a clutch of O-levels and a grade 1 CSE in technical drawing. To the total consternation of my exasperated parents, I managed to completely waste ten years of perfectly adequate state education in daydreaming, mucking around and generally playing the fool. (Ironically, one of my daughters, Juliette, is a secondary school teacher now.) Unsurprisingly, I never attended university, but I did attend Cranfield Business School in 2007 and completed their SME Business Growth Programme, which was of great benefit.

For many years I was in the fashion business where I came across such luminaries as Sir Philip Green, who taught me a thing or two about negotiating. I built a worldwide leather clothing brand called Muubaa, which is now run by my daughter, Georgia. During the years when I was growing Muubaa, I travelled extensively, clocking up two foreign trips per week in one year as I built distribution in 30 different countries across the world whilst managing production in South Asia and the Far East.

I also created and sold a furnishings and linen business and was heavily involved in my own logistics business, where we handled distribution for a number of other wholesale businesses. At the end of 2016, I exited my last business and decided that I would like to market my experience rather than jump straight back into the frying pan again myself. So I founded Funding Nav as an advisory and broking boutique aimed at helping entrepreneurs create more cash for themselves and for their businesses, because it's something I wish I'd had access too when I was building trading businesses.

Since then, I've been involved with numerous different businesses and have managed to add value in every case.

Sectors include food and beverage, leisure and hospitality, fashion, marketing, telecoms, tech and medicine.

I've noticed commonality across all sectors, which is generally down to the fact that, in SME businesses, the leader is expected to be a jack of all trades. This is, of course, an impossibility. Also, the business becomes almost an extension of the owner to the extent that business issues quickly manifest themselves physically.

I have read and listened to a lot of business books in my time and I've found that most of them contain very few new ideas, lack any kind of humour whatsoever, and are often highly repetitive as they struggle to fill the pages with sufficient words to justify the cover price. So I've tried hard to make this one snappy, readable, to the point and actionable, and have used off-the-wall examples to prove my points.

Given that I'm married to the very patient Harriet, with whom I have four daughters all still at home at the time of writing, Georgia, Juliette, Milly and Josie, I have huge motivation to both get out of the house every morning and to earn a decent living. It ain't cheap and it ain't peaceful living with five women, I can tell you!

I welcome your feedback to stephen.sacks@fundingnav.com.

Acknowledgements

I would like to thank my wife, Harriet for dragging me away to the dullest place on earth for Christmas 2017 that also had terrible internet connectivity. No question that this provided me with the ideal environment to unload 35 years of commercial experience onto the written page over a couple of weeks.

I would also like to thank her for her often brutal honesty which I frankly should have sometimes listened to more attentively.

Having worked side by side with my dad for 30 years, he undoubtedly inspired me massively and it is ironic that I only took up writing after he died, as he would certainly have had a point of view that I would love to have heard.

Mr Janes was the teacher who made the biggest impact on me at school and perhaps was responsible for shaping my later career in finance.

I would also like to thank everyone I have engaged with commercially throughout my career, as I gained more knowledge and experience from every interaction. And I would like to apologise to all those I've upset on the way. I was fortunate to have a trading relationship with Sir Philip Green back in the day and he was undeniably an inspiration.

Finally, thank you to my A team (literally); my distributor Alex, my editor Alexa and especially my publisher (also called) Alexa.